Retur
The Void

How to achieve success through times
of adversity, loss, fear and challenge!

Joanna Knight

First published in 2011 by:

Live It Publishing
27 Old Gloucester Road
London, United Kingdom.
WC1N 3AX
www.liveitpublishing.com

Publisher's Note

Although every effort has been made to ensure the accuracy of the information, advice and instructions contained in this book, it is sold with the understanding that neither the author nor the publisher are giving specific diagnostic or treatment advice.

Each person has unique needs and circumstances that can present complex issues that are beyond the scope of this book. For specific advice, the reader is advised to consult a professional coach or therapist.

ISBN 978-1-906954-29-1 (pbk)

I would like to thank the love of my family and friends for being there when the darkness contained no light.

Contents

Foreword

I get requests to write forewords for peoples' books all the time and most I have to sadly say not to, as there are only so many forewords a chap can write without things getting silly. However along the way, I've met people who I encouraged to write a book, either because they had a lot to say, or a big need to say something. Some of these I've even helped to get publishing deals. But it's hard to write a book. I've written 16 myself (14 of these published), so I know: the loneliness of sitting there, the doubts that creep in as you're writing, the rewrites and corrections that take as long as writing it in the first place, and then the convoluted process of actually getting the book out there all neat and tidy between its covers.

Normally I'd write a foreword because I'm so taken by the artfulness of writing style or the originality of the material. The reason I've done so for this book is for neither of these but to honor Joanna's incredible persistence and willingness to see the project through, simple as that. For I believe that, narrative aside, somehow she manages to transmit the essence of this most crucial quality of perseverance, and that this will bring you great benefits.

Barefoot Doctor

Introduction

*H*aving dealt with a multitude of negative challenges throughout many areas of my life, in this book I will share my unique insight into the human ability to conquer adversity and face these trials at a level that can only enhance self-growth and success.

As a trained Clinical Hypnotherapist with an intuitive knowledge of the human condition, I hope to share with you, not only my own personal methods of coping and lifestyle improvement, but also my professional knowledge that has grown over the years.

It is my wish that all those who have given up, lost hope, or are just plain tired of losing, are encouraged by this book, inspired and directed to a better life that is full of promise, direction and renewed zest. At the end of each chapter you will find a powerful affirmation to practise saying either out loud, or to review each day, along with some useful note space for your own private thoughts and reflection.

Enjoy!

CHAPTER 1

Taking stock

Reflection and note:
it's ok to make mistakes

> "A life without mistakes is a life paralysed
> by fear and stilted growth."
> J. A. Knight, therapist, author, philosopher, 2009

Over the course of my life, I have made my fair share of mistakes, some of which I regret, and others (on reflection) that I don't. But what is our definition or perception of a mistake? Is it to ignore advice that we have been given by a loved one? Could a mistake be something we blame on past emotions and conditioning, which affects our decision making, and leads to an unwanted outcome? Or it is it a mistake to fail to see another person's point of view, and think of ourselves as simply selfish? Could it be that we are just bad at decision making, because we are naïve or immature?

All in all, the hows, whys and whens of any mistake are of little consolation once the mistake has been made. After all, once we have made an error of judgement, or have acted inappropriately, there is no taking it back, and of course that is something that we just have to learn to live with, and accept. Or is it?

Living with the consequences of a mistake that affects others as well as ourselves can be tough, especially when we feel responsible, or that others are judging and blaming us for that mistake. The pain and embarrassment of getting it wrong can lead us into all sorts of problems in the future, such as low self-esteem, beating ourselves up because we simply won't forgive ourselves for what we have done, or even carrying issues around into future relationships, whether they are work relationships, or any other kind of relationship. In extreme cases, we may even begin to believe that we are undeserving and may become depressed because of the consequences of our actions.

The point here is to understand that to make a mistake is actually quite normal. It's something that happens in life – always has, always will. If you have done something that in your view is truly terrible just ask yourself 'Was it my intention to upset my life, and everyone else's around me?', 'Did I predict the outcome?', 'Would I have enjoyed this outcome?' and 'Would I make the same choices again, or in the same fashion?' I think you will have your answer. Let's take a look at the following example and see what we can learn from how someone's intention can affect the outcome.

An unhappy wife has left her husband for another man, due to a variety of unresolved issues, and years of built up frustrations and inner resentment. She is shocked by her own behaviour and considers it to be out of character, but quite clearly she has reached breaking point. She has taken her children with her for a new life full of what she sees as fresh possibility and she hopes for happiness.

However, just a couple of days later she finds herself returning the children to her now ex-partner for a weekend. She does this to show that she is not without feeling, but also due to sheer guilt, a sense of obligation, confusion and various other factors. She can relate only too well to how it feels to be hurt and let down because of her own past hurts within the marriage.

This woman believes that by showing her willingness to share and be reasonable, she will make the blow of infidelity a little less painful. So she then arranges to collect her children a few days later, hoping things may have had time to settle down and the situation will have had time to become clear.

After those few days have passed however, she finds herself on the telephone to a hugely distraught husband who wants to have the children for just a day or so more. She reluctantly agrees, knowing all too well that he is hoping she will return, as he still wants her to come home, but in the back of her mind, she also realises that realistically with a full time job and a house now to keep, he could not possibly look after two children, and so her mind is put at ease, for the time being at least.

However, a short while later on her return to the family home, to her shock she finds that the front door lock has been changed, and she is told that the children's school is now under the strong impression that she has indeed abandoned them. To make things worse, rumour now has it that her mental state and behaviour are questionable and as she does not live at the home address anymore, she may attempt to kidnap her own children. To her despair she finds that the playground is guarded at home time, and she experiences various judgmental looks from what appears to be, dubious local mums on watch. She can't get anywhere near her children, or take them home with her, for fear of reprisal and the legal consequences.

While still in a state of shock, she then learns that she has lost all her legal rights in leaving the family home, and should instead have kicked her husband out to maintain her rights. She hadn't realised that such events might occur, or of the consequences of her actions. Naturally this woman doesn't want to cause a public scene, and she doesn't wish to cause further upset to her children, or to make the matter a physical fight. She decides instead to take a mature stance, to rise above it all and take the whole matter to court, where she has faith that everything will be sorted out and reconsidered fairly and equally.

Sadly, with lengthy time delays and much continued fighting, stress, and expense, she eventually loses her case, as it is deemed that the children are more settled at their original home and school, and not with their mother. The final devastating result sees her losing her children, her home, her dignity and her sense of self respect.

During this testing time, the woman had come to the realisation that her life had become rather like a game of chess. Every move she made had to be carefully considered, and every word she spoke was under the scrutiny of her ex-husband and his solicitors. If someone decides to start a rumour, then the effect can be quite damaging, even when no one really knows the truth, after all, some people take the view that there is no smoke without fire. As a result this woman found herself wrapped up in what amounted to a modern day witch-hunt, and this was carried out quite unbelievably in the 21st century.

So, was she stupid? Did she deserve the outcome? What would you have done in her place? Was it her intention to hurt herself, her children, and her future? Absolutely not. We have returned to the intention behind the action we touched upon above. Yes, perhaps she was foolish (and she definitely wasn't up to date with the law), but the important point to grasp is that she didn't purposely wake up one morning and think, 'I know, today I will make my life a living hell, and ruin the lives of my children and deny myself a future with them in the process'.

You may be wondering how I can be so sure of this woman's feelings: simply because I was that woman.

Yes, it was me, and a mistake that I paid most highly for. Did I hurt myself in the process? I can safely say yes. Did I beat myself up for being so soft, so naïve, so utterly stupid and emotionally irrational? Absolutely. Would I change anything if I could reverse time, with my renewed wisdom and hindsight? Yes. But as it is impossible to turn back time, and I have made many changes to my life since, there isn't anything else I can actually do to change what happened. Or is there a way, that on reflection, I could review it with new eyes, and with my own future success and progression in mind.

In early 2002 I was in a very different place from where I am today. I had managed to lose my children, my home, my possessions, and my car, along with my dignity and self-respect. As a result, eventually I began to experience health problems. In addition to all of this I had the unfortunate experience of attending four family funerals over the next two years. Life at that time was at an all-time low and I didn't yet know my job would be the next thing to go.

I had no money , I was homeless, and I had only one bin liner full of clothes, and with this much strain in my life I had to find somewhere new to live. I had to literally re-arrange my life in my late thirties. For the first time in my life I was totally alone. I was on a mission of self-punishment, and had even left the new relationship I was in, due to my many conflicting emotions of self-blame, guilt and shame.

During this time I had to face many of my demons, but face them I did, head on in fact, and today I have a business, an apartment I can be proud of, a loving relationship (yes with the original guy I wanted to be with), good health, and best of all I have a good, loving relationship with both my kids.

Before we continue, I need to explain that it is not my intention for this book to be all about me: in fact this book was written by me for you, and will therefore happily focus on you. I have simply used my real life experience with its wisdom, maturity and knowledge that cannot always be taken from chalkboards, school lessons, demonstrations or guess work. Some things in life just need to be experienced first-hand..

The turning point for me during this massive life challenge was in taking stock. This empowering notion involves literally noting down and taking responsibility for what has passed. It's about learning as much as you can not only from the situation, but ultimately about yourself.

You see, when you lose everything you can either sink or swim. For those who try to swim, there can also be an extremely enlightening experience: a deep sense of inner freedom. Hitting rock bottom can be intensely liberating. In that instant you become quite fearless, almost dangerously free. Life can't hurt you any more, and that knowledge is the key to your inner strength, your inner survivor, and the inner lioness that rears her beautiful head.

So, let's look at you. If for instance you have done something in your life that you feel ashamed of, or just can't quite forgive yourself for, just take a look at our earlier questions again and ask yourself, 'Was the outcome, my intention?' 'Did I intend to arrive where I am today as a result?' 'If I'd known what the outcome would be, would I have carried on in the same direction, or in the same fashion?' I would wager that your answer would be a firm NO.

Next, if you have made a mistake you regret, just take a few moments to yourself, and note down on a pad the process of HOW and WHY you made your decision. Just look at the situation with honest eyes. See your choices from a higher, more detached perspective and the circumstances that drove those choices forward, then note down what feelings led to those choices.

If you're a little stuck here is a short example using the aforementioned situation.

My past mistake was returning my children to my ex-partner and being naïve as to the law and consequences of my actions. With the benefit of hindsight I should have revised my rights, and acted accordingly.

Why did I make that foolish decision? Because I FELT (remember the emotions here) guilt, fear, and shame, and by appearing to be reasonable, I thought would result in better communications and a peaceful outcome. That fear and guilt drove my irrational choice. I felt guilty for what I had done, and feared that others would judge me if I didn't show that I was prepared to be fair about the situation. I also wanted to show balance to the children. Those were the circumstances and feelings that drove my choices.

You can do this exercise too to get to the bottom of your own decisions, and to notice and learn that your choices are in fact not always stupid, selfish or as bad as you may think. Reflection is a wonderful tool and, if approached positively, can show us so much more than we could ever have realised.

Next take an honest and loving look at what you have written, almost as if you were a trusted friend scanning over your best friend's notes with a mood for offering a fair, loving and objective viewpoint. The reason I ask this of you, is to teach you to recognise the emotions that were involved, by staying in simple and calm detachment. Take notice of what mood or emotion really stands out in any of the statements you have written down.

I want you to look at WHY that particular emotion came up, and what stirred it. Look at HOW that emotion drove you to your choice? For instance, if you were a talented singer, but were shy and fearful about approaching the X-Factor auditions, then that feeling may have driven you to stage fright, or to running away from the situation, or even not applying for it. There you have the outcome of that emotional reaction.

Lastly, I want you to take note of what emotion would have placed you in a more positive state of mind, and that could have produced a better choice or outcome. You could even use this exercise for something going on in your life right now.

Once again, here is a short example from my experience to help you.

My own guilt was fuelled by knowing how it felt to have been cheated on by someone else, and how others judge those who cheat. My fear was of taking responsibility for what I had done, and this in turn left me feeling disempowered and uncertain.

A better range of emotions would have been calmness, self-belief and forgiveness, which would have given me more control and detachment from my emotional situation. These positive emotions would have helped with clarity and rational judgement and I could have been at peace with my choice. I could also have read a self-help book, or taken a stress management course, had some hypnosis, practised yoga, deep breathing, detachment or any other tool that may have produced a more controlled and clear vision for myself.

I could have chosen to be more assertive, and in calmly stating my choice, I would have been less inclined to have rushed into making a rash decision. I would have seen things more clearly, and given myself time to inwardly process the situation. It would also have given my ex-partner time to take responsibility for his own feelings,

Hopefully once you have completed your own notes and the exercises above you will have a better understanding of your own emotional drivers, moods and anxieties. You will recognise that fear on some level, could have driven you to irrational behaviour, and that you can now choose to view the situation from a different perspective in the future.

The good news is that there are lots of ways we can learn to achieve calmness, self-belief and clarity – either by attending a relaxation course, meditating, reading a self-help book, practising a discipline or taking some simple reflective exercises.

What I have discovered on my journey is this: if others judge you harshly right now it is simply because they have chosen to label you. Some people feel safe when they have a label for something. This gives them a sense of knowledge and power, and can feed their ego at the same time.

However, when you are unfairly judged just remember that

the label of bad mother, lazy or selfish, or mentally unstable, is only a descriptive of another person's perception, and is not always a truth. The only one who knows the real truth is the person who is going through the experience at the time.

So give yourself a big pat on the back, as you have taken the first step towards some truly positive action – in buying this book, taking stock of your situation, being responsible for yourself by noting down your emotional drivers, and giving yourself some valuable nuggets of wisdom along the way.

From this day forwards I will rest in the knowledge that I am only human, and it is ok for me to make mistakes.

I am safe.

Notes

CHAPTER 2

Gaining through the pain

Seeing the light, welcoming the genius

> *Life shrinks or expands in proportion to one's courage.*
> Anais Nin, French Novelist 1903-1977

I expect you have heard the term 'no pain, no gain'. It's a term generally used in relation to physical activity or weight loss and in many ways is true – by exerting ourselves or trying hard we can experience benefits, or gains.

When we want to succeed in a particular career, it is a case of study, work hard, make time sacrifices, and enjoy success having developed yourself to your full potential. When entering a serious relationship that we desperately want to work, it is sometimes essential to make certain sacrifices such as moving to another area away from family and friends, or giving up your flat, or even your beloved pet if your other half suffers from allergies.

In a similar way, if an investor wants to make as much money as possible, he will be prepared to take a risk on the stock market, and sometimes there is loss, sometimes a reward.

The point I am trying to make is that life does not come with a cast iron guarantee against shortfall, disappointment, loss or failure. Deep down we all know this, but sometimes we can live in denial of it, simply because it is an unpleasant reminder of what can go wrong.

Life is not only about survival, but also experience. Those who are willing to play their cards and fully experience life will appreciate the highs so much more than the lows, for light can be better appreciated when it has been cast against darkness and disappointment in life.

Let's imagine a perfect world, just for a moment, where we wake up every morning and the sun is always shining. Everyone is content and smiling, children are happily playing, and people set about their daily tasks without a single moan or gripe. The earth is run by one harmonious universal party with no opposition. There are no wars, disputes, or differences over religion.

Everyone receives a top quality education, and then has a choice of a wide variety of jobs to suit their natural gift or interests. Rewards are equal, and all citizens take full responsibility for their own families. Each person is included in society and no one is ever lonely.

Each day runs without a single hitch and at bedtime we all sleep like babies, dreaming the sweetest of dreams, in the most comfortable of homes. As a result our health is always optimized, and every morning we are all refreshed, youthful, energized and raring to go. Wow, just imagine that!

Now, picture that same scene running over and over a hundred, two hundred or even a thousand years later. It never rains, the sun always shines, as every day is more or less the same. Children are extremely content, and do exactly as they are asked. Everyone stays in one constant happy and beautiful state of mind. Although life is peaceful, it remains in a state of guaranteed safe expectancy. Jobs are the same, day in day out, as they are fitted to each individual. Everyone is on an equal footing.

Now ask yourself this: where is human excellence truly harnessed? Does it thrive in generation after generation going down the same path, doing the same old thing over and over again? Or does it flourish with personal growth, opportunity, adversity, diversity, opposition, challenge and courage? If life was perfect every day for the next 100 years, perhaps you would get bored. You could wake up one morning, and want to be just a little rebellious in some way. You might feel stilted, suffocated or limited. You might miss the challenge of stretching yourself, measuring yourself to others as a barometer.

I am not saying that peacefulness isn't a good thing, in fact I am a spiritual person. There are many times when my imagination runs away with me, to where I live in an idealist society. But I wonder if we would actually like it, if we had it. I think we'd miss moaning once in a while; or those lazy days, when we just want to lounge around and not care; or getting soaked because it poured down with rain for a change; or eating naughty food and getting a little merry on a drink or two; having a hearty debate with someone who disagrees with us; changing our career; or expressing our own unique style of dress.

The important point is that although life isn't ideal, it is what you make of it given the situation you find yourself in at the time. At times of course we all make mistakes, but challenges and difficult situations (that arise through our own mistakes, or not) can awaken the deepest, wisest part of us. That wisdom is in our own resourcefulness, courage, determination, focus, resilience and motivation – it is a brilliant fragment of our own emotional intelligence that we do not always realise we have on a daily basis.

So how can we gain through the pain and difficulties of any adverse circumstances? And what exactly are we gaining? Does it depend on the situation, on us, or maybe both? The answer my friends, is deep within you, because you are the one who holds the answers to your own wants, desires and needs. We already know the answers, as did our ancestors who faced more immediate challenges and harsh realities, but we just need a little reminding now and then.

If your world suddenly came crashing down around you (or maybe it already has) and you had serious debts, had lost your home and all of your possessions, your reputation and then to top it all off, you had a death or two in the family, you would probably be in a very dark place. This is a natural and acceptable reaction, and many people who care for you would understand.

During these times of challenge, after the truth of the situation has had time to sink in, we tend to eventually go deep within ourselves for comfort and answers. We may analyse the situation, and over time we may come out of that dark hole with a new perspective, and inner strength that we simply didn't possess before. Experience always shines a new light onto an old problem.

However, unfortunately some of us can sink even deeper into that hole, and go into self-blame or maybe guilt or shame mode, and to some extent that is also a natural process, when it comes to grief for instance. But if we were to choose to deal with every challenging situation in such a way, and stay in that frame of mind, then what would the end result be? It is unlikely there would be anything to gain from remaining in such a dark place. After all, every positive or negative experience in life is just that: an experience. In turn, this kind of challenge gives us all a chance to face whatever is being presented to us, and to ultimately learn from it.

So, next time when you are faced with an undesirable challenge, why not take a different approach, and accept the experience which is being presented to you. I wouldn't expect you to jump for joy at the thought of a dreadful piece of news, but you can choose to react to that challenge in a different way and in doing so you can change the outcome.

For instance, some people can adopt such a self-secured mindset that in times of trouble they will simply go into a 'poor me' way of thinking. Of course we will tend to lick our wounds in order to feel better, but if we overindulge in our own personal 'pity party' after a while, no one will want to come.

In the past, one of the most important things I have learnt is never to sink into the pity mode for too long, if you can help it. Yes, I accept that this is a hard thing to do, but let's be really honest here: 'poor me', is an unattractive state of mind. We become the helpless victim, and disempower ourselves, from our own perspective and from everyone else's too! Most people are willing to help, but it will only be a matter of time before everyone becomes uninterested in someone who is constantly wrapped up in their own on-going drama. Ultimately these people can also be unfairly labelled as attention seekers.

As harsh as this may sound, it is a truth my friends. We can only expect to take so much time and resources from another, before that other person becomes drained and bored. Once we have had time to come to terms with our challenge, then we have the choice to shed our hurt and disappointment, and shine some of our own wisdom, strength and light onto the situation.

So, let's take a good look at what you are presented with right now, and see how we can remove the emotion from it, by viewing it from a more empowering perspective using our good friend logic. Logic involves detachment, and can be quite a comfort, as it provides us with simple structure and simple truth. If you are upset, yes, deal with that emotion and cry as much as you like, stamp your feet, or go for a long run, whatever floats your emotional boat, but don't allow that emotion to create havoc all over your day, week, or month after that.

Some counsellors or psychological experts may disagree or object to the above methods, but it is not my suggestion to avoid dealing with your emotion. What I am saying however is to simply be aware of becoming 'stuck' in an on-going destructive emotional cycle.

Self-awareness plays a key part in self-progression, and in turn that growth comes from becoming self-aware! I guarantee that applying logic and detachment to certain situations works as I have used this method many times myself, and have helped others to do the same.

If you are in a particular situation, you may have made the

effort to view it with clear, cool and logical eyes. To do this, you may wish to make a list based on fact, or view your situation in the same way as a very dear friend would – with calm detachment. As a result you may suddenly see your situation with more clarity and focus, especially when you have given your emotional being time to rest and settle down a little.

For example, let's take a man who has lost his job of ten years or so, through redundancy, and at which he has worked very hard. As a result, his emotional being is obviously upset for many reasons:

- He may have worked hard to reach the level at which he specialises, and this may be specific to his field.
- His may not be able to get a new job at his current wage and so he may fear a lower standard of living.
- He may worry that his age is now a further obstacle for him to overcome at future interviews.
- His ego may also be hurt because his sense of pride and achievement was also wrapped up in his work.
- He may miss the social element of working with his colleagues of ten years, and so on...

With so many negative emotions and concerns it is no wonder that this man may well end up feeling worse than he already does, even though these concerns may not hold any truth to them.

If he continues to focus on the emotional drivers of worry and concern for his future, he is lending himself little opportunity for growth. If he chooses to see the situation with calm logic then he opens himself up to cool clarity and vision.

What follows is an example of how this man can apply logical calm thinking and the resultant comfort it can bring.

- First of all, I accept that I am not the first, nor will I be the last to lose my job through no fault of my own. My company simply did not foresee the solutions to the problems they now face.
- I have reached a level within my field, and so have proved to myself that I can do it again. I therefore already know that I am capable and intelligent, and can achieve future goals.
- In being able to apply myself, I know that there is every possibility that I can earn a good wage, simply because I now have the experience, wisdom and attitude to succeed.
- My age could work to my advantage, as someone younger could not have possibly achieved as much as I have, plus I have years of experience within other areas behind me.
- I have always taken pride in my work, and will do so again because that is just me. I have a good track record to prove this.
- I look forward to this new stage in my life; it was about time for me to move forwards anyway. This will give me the chance to challenge myself, and meet new, fresh and interesting people.
- I have always taken responsibility for myself, and I am happy to do so again, because I am adaptable and capable.

Having calm clarity gives us a new chance to come in from a position of strength, responsibility and focus. When we have focus, we are not deceived in any way. We are facing up to the truth, and when we are facing truth, we are no longer in denial; instead we are on the path to wisdom and self-empowerment!

For me, it was one of those magical moments when I had finally accepted my situation for what it was, nothing more and nothing less. I faced up to my mistakes, and took responsibility for my own feelings, and in that moment my perception became crystal clear.

When we experience thoughts such as 'I'm not good enough' or 'I could never do that' we are sentencing ourselves to a life that constantly lacks something. However, by turning those negatives thoughts around, we can live with power, and think renewed thoughts that will serve us in a positive way. So, why not think 'I am good enough to do anything that I really want to do' or 'I can achieve what I want, when I choose to focus on it.'

The light within the challenge you are now faced with is a clear understanding of your own situation and all that is being presented to you, with your own willing acceptance of the truth. You see, there is nothing wrong with emotion at all, but as a hypnotherapist I would advise that emotions need to be felt, dealt with, and faced up to. If we become caught up in a constant state of negative emotion, then over time our sense of clear thinking can become severely blocked, resulting in irrational judgements, or hasty mistakes driven by fear that we may later regret. This is why I would recommend that you choose to feel and accept your pain for it is a natural part of being human. Once you have accepted your pain, you can then walk your way through that foggy feeling, until you reach a clearing of strong calm logic, detachment, and a field full of focus!

As a final word, if you are still unsure as to how to come into a state of acceptance of your situation, or you feel you can't quite face up to it right now, then seeking out a qualified therapist, or quietly using affirmations can be of great help. Try this affirmation below to start with:

*From this day
forwards I choose to accept
my situation with calmness,
truth and logic.
I am free to release my
emotions and move on.
I am always safe.*

Notes

CHAPTER 3

Overriding the fear, finding your truth

Getting to know you,
dealing with opposition

> *Resolve to be thyself: and know that he who*
> *finds himself, loses his misery.*
> Matthew Arnold, British writer, 1822-1888

It's funny how we take for granted that we know ourselves, and yet it isn't until we are faced with severe adversity and challenge, that we can take a firm stance on who we really are. In a way it's a home coming for many, and armed with this knowledge we can find what meaning and focus we have to offer, not only to others, but to ourselves.

When we gain from sometimes painful experiences, we arrive at our own truth. Truth is about honesty in taking responsibility for what fulfils us, and what doesn't. It is a brave move to be true to yourself, but a rewarding one all the same.

When we look back at how far we have come, we can begin to look at the human experience that is unique to us, and be proud of what we have achieved. If someone else has dealt with a situation in a certain way, it doesn't mean that their particular way of dealing with it, is right for us. Each and every one of us has our own inner pattern, our own way of reaching our goal, target or agenda in life, given the experiences we have had to date or the people we have met. In short, there is neither a right nor a wrong

In life, there will be many times when we have to face up to fear. Fear of not liking what we find in ourselves, fear of others or new circumstances, fear of anything in fact, so lets just take a quick look at this fascinating subject, fear.

First, we need to go back a few million years, to where the root of our ancestral survival began, back in the cave, back to a time where just staying alive was an everyday task, and danger was something to be faced with respect, speed and instinct.

Many of us have heard about the 'fight or flight' response, and indeed it is my theory that there is also a third 'freeze' response. The situation we find ourselves in, and our personality type will heavily influence our ultimate response. If for instance a sabre tooth tiger came into a cave, and it was blocking your escape, you would have three choices based upon your fear/survival response within the few seconds of seeing the threat. The first choice for many would be to run, but of course run where? The second choice would be to fight, but fight with what? The third choice could be to freeze, giving yourself a few precious seconds to think, or at least to not to entice a large cat whose instinct is largely based upon movement.

Actually the outcome is irrelevant here, as it is the fear response we are interested in. How does this apply to a modern day scenario, such as working in an office with an irritating boss? Amazingly enough, those same base survival responses from the depths of our unconscious mind, are lurking and working just fine, along with many various subconscious fears, that have been pre-programmed in us from various outside sources, since childhood. Unconscious responses, and subconscious pre-programmed responses can become crossed and confused, and so a seemingly unthreatening scenario, may become a big deal if your subconscious mind can't tell the difference between the two. The problem here is that within the world of the subconscious mind, a situation is either black or white, as there is no grey. In other words, an experience is either totally cool and unthreatening, or completely terrifying. So if we experience a response that is still lurking in our subconscious, we can't consciously do anything physical about it. Instead, we have to ignore our pushed stress buttons, bite our tongue and continue to act as professionally as we can.

We soon realise that we can't just hit out at our boss for instance (the fight response), which may be the natural instinct for some. Being stuck in a frustrating traffic jam can also raise the fear response, as the fear is connected to being late for work, being humiliated in front of colleagues, wrongly judged, or even fear of losing our job. Again, within the dynamics of a personal relationship, we can hold inner frustration for fear of losing our partner, or fail to reprimand our children for fear of them not loving us enough, or eventually abandoning us.

Today this fear isn't labelled as simple base fear, but with the very fashionable word 'stress'. These days stress is everywhere: in the divorce courts; in traffic jams; at work; at home with your kids who won't help when you need to just get things done; when we find ourselves in a relationship that we aren't quite sure of. I could go on, but I'm sure I don't need to, as you have probably got a whole list of your own.

Naturally, we all have our own unique coping mechanisms for such circumstances, but you may not like how you respond when under pressure. If your personality type won't fight, or freeze, but would prefer to flee, this may cause you continued frustration. Or perhaps you always fight, and would rather freeze out the situation, to give you time to think, and cool off.

The good news is that despite our different personality types, and our past or current conditioning, we can just decide to change, and see that transition through. You own your own power, we all do. If you are an adult, with a working brain, and a voice, then you can make choices and lots of them too. So, when you decide to challenge yourself and your own personality traits, then there is absolutely nothing that can stop you except yourself.

Change is nothing to fear, it is a natural way of life, and if you are still questioning that, try looking at it like this. Change is inevitable, and is something to explore, to grow from, to learn from, and to even get a little excited about. After all, have you ever seen a small child who doesn't want to try something new? It's about experience, it's about learning, and it's all a healthy part of normal life.

If you are now standing on the platform of life, waiting to get on that train, and change your perception, your circumstances, or even your destination, then there is nothing more rewarding than knowing yourself and your fears, and facing your fears anyway. As it says in the Good Book 'Fear knocked at the door, faith answered, but no one was there'.

But how do we overcome the fear of change? Most of us have to be occasionally nudged in the direction of change, as most people prefer the familiar, the known, the comfort zone of our own little world. But if we never dip our big toe into the ocean, we will never know if we like it or not. This is why it is so important to find your 'adaption zone', where flexibility becomes your friend.

Now, if you have had a few hard knocks or challenges in life, you will probably know, that it changes you from the inside out. Over the years, our view of the world alters slightly each time we experience a setback, and it is up to us to decide if that setback is going to knock us over and defeat us, or stabilize us with unique inner wisdom, self-acceptance, strength and increased perception.

The scales Part 1

To make this point clear, I want you to now visualize a traditional pair of scales, just like those depicted by the sign of Libra, or by justice. These scales can illustrate any aspect of life. Most of the time, we rarely sit on the middle of those scales, but instead favour one side more than the other one side, depending at what stage in life we are at.

There are two ways that we can use these scales in an exercise. Firstly let's find out a little about your comfort zone. I want you to note down, or imagine that the right side of the scales is love and relationships, and that the left is money and material success. I am not judging, and neither should you, as remember there is no right or wrong. We are simply looking at where you are comfortable on the scales in relation to these two aspects of life. This can be a good indicator as to why certain things aren't working out for you within certain areas of your life.

I want you to be totally honest with yourself, and view the most comfortable place for you to sit. Perhaps you sit a little closer to the right with love, people, and relationships. Or you may sit a little closer to the left with money, career and material things. Either way, different things take priority in people's lives, but the most important thing is to be completely honest with yourself.

If you are sitting over to the left, and are wondering why your love life isn't taking off for instance, you may well have your answer, as your point of focus and comfort is with money and career. If you are sitting far over to the right and you have no money, once again you can see that your energies are aimed mainly at relationships, which is why money is secondary.

Although it may sound obvious, once we see the plain truth on paper, or even within our mind's eye, we can then take responsible steps to correct any area in life that holds disappointment for us. If however you are perfectly happy and completely comfortable sitting where you are, then good for you!

The scales Part 2

The second part of this lovely little exercise has been designed by me, to help you identify your own current way of living, and in doing so you will be able to clearly see what has been holding you back until now.

First, pick a subject which is affecting you currently. This could be a health issue, love or family issue, money and debts, housing, work and employment, travel, spirituality or whatever comes to mind.

Ok, that's great. Now as I can't read your mind, I will set a simple example against the background of the most common subject in my therapy room which is 'relationship anxiety'. Please remember this is just an example, so you can use your subject as you please and along the same lines, all you have to do is ask slightly different questions.

Let's imagine that I have a broken long-term relationship and I am upset and stressed by this. I am feeling pretty low, and extremely challenged at this time, and when I look to my emotions I may well begin to identify with feelings such as abandonment, insecurity, fear, anger and loneliness.

Now I want you to do the same for yourself and your chosen subject. If for instance money and debt are troubling you, how are you feeling? Is it worry, fear, anxiety, or do you feel victimised? Or if it is a health issue you could be feeling uncertain, afraid, alone, or weak. You decide, given your circumstances.

To the far left of my scales is where my inner fear lies, and to the right is where love and acceptance resides. Remember, whatever subject you choose to examine, the left is always the negative, and the right is the positive.

To the left is where anxiety, fear of the unknown, fear of being alone, guilt, self-blame, shame, denial, anger, resistance to change and any other negative you can think of.

To the right is where love, acceptance, healing, patience, tranquillity, calm, clarity, freedom of expression, creativity, joy, happiness and fun reside, plus any other positive you can imagine.

Now at this particular stage in your life, and given your present circumstances, work out where you tend to sit on those scales. Also most importantly where do you 'think' you should be sitting? If you are sitting a little more to the left than you realised, I want you to ask yourself the following questions:

- Is this the right place for me to be sitting right now?
- How will this place that I choose to sit (yes, choose to sit) serve my future?
- If I continue to stay sitting where I am, will things change for the better, or will they stay the same as before?
- Is it easy to stay sitting where I am because it is familiar?
- If so, does this feel comfortable for me?
- Am I choosing this area to sit, just because I always have before? Is this a habit, because this is all I know?

Not all of these questions may fit your situation, but for the ones that do, just see if you can answer them honestly and directly.

When you are ready, take a look at what answers you have, and examine the 'belief' behind those answers. If you need to make a list at this point, that is fine. Jot it all down while you make yourself a nice cuppa... and we can start turning these negatives around.

- If you are sitting close to fear, what is it exactly that you are afraid of, and why?
- If your fear is loneliness, do you believe that loneliness is a bad thing? If so why is that?

- If you are sitting close to insecurity, what makes you feel insecure?
- If it is guilt that you sit next to, what purpose does that guilt serve? And what would life be like without that guilt?
- If you believe that guilt is important on your value scale, are you setting your own values for yourself a shade too high? And would you expect another person to hold the same high moral values as you? Would you be so unforgiving of them?
- Do you believe in constantly reminding others of their faults? If not, why would you do this to yourself?

Once you have taken a look and answered some of these questions for yourself, you will have a clearer understanding of where you choose to sit on the scales and why. The clever thing here is that now you can see it, you can take steps to positive change!

To further illustrate how damaging a negative inner dialogue with yourself can be, just take a peek into this imaginary journey:

For years now, you have had the most wonderful loyal friend who has always been there for you. They manage to get you out of bed on time most mornings; they even enjoy preparing a bath for you; they cook for you, feed you, and are happy to make you a drink; they take you shopping and choose clothes for you; they read to you and even tuck you in before bed. Every day they take care of you, look out for you, manage your diary for the next day. This friend has done this for you, year after year, without complaint, and yet...

On one particular day your friend makes a few mistakes along the way. Perhaps they have entered a wrong date in your diary, spilt hot tea on your lap, or embarrassed you by accident. Now ask yourself what your reaction would be. Would you call them names, scream at them? Would you unfairly rate them against the performance of others, and compare them with other best friends? Would you scorn them? Even make fun of them? Surely, after all those years of steadfast loyalty, and hard work, I would doubt it, and yet...

This best friend we have been referring to is YOU. You are the one who does everything for you, day after day, week after week, month after month, and year after year. Despite this however, most of us have an inner dialogue that is a combination of on-going negative and self-destructive talk.

This self-induced abuse can go on repeat cycle for years and years, and so, guess what? Your loyal friend simply gives up on you, in other words you begin to give up on yourself. And can we really blame that part of ourselves that feels so unappreciated, so hurt, so upset? I don't think so.

If there is enough repeated negative input, someday very soon, if not already, part of you will give up trying to achieve, or taking pride, or seeing what success you have had, rather than what you haven't. Have you ever thought where that self-critique comes from I wonder? Could it be a voice from your past? Or a frightening experience? You have the power to find that answer, and change your mind from today!

So before we come to the end of this chapter, make a simple list of all your successes, your achievements, positive experiences, and the days that have been the happiest for you. Keep that list close, for whenever you need a little reminder of just how far you have come, and why you are still standing here today.

And for those of you that may be thinking 'well actually I haven't achieved much, as I haven't experienced much', or 'I don't know what happiness is?' how about acknowledging your efforts by noticing how you continue to get yourself out of bed early in the mornings for work; for taking the time to read this book; for keeping yourself clean and presentable; for passing your driving test (however long it may have taken); for keeping your home organised; for taking the effort to make decent friends over the years; having your first child; for learning a new skill or passing an exam; for being a responsible pet owner or even growing your own cabbages. And most of all for being a survivor.

In other words my friend, there is always something in life that we can be proud of, be thankful for, and feel a sense of achievement and happiness from, whatever it may be. So let your mind run wild, and start being truly proud of yourself from today, because no one is quite like you!

From this day forwards
I have faith in the comfort
of getting to know me.
I approve of myself, and
choose to own my own power
from this moment on.
I am a work in perfect
progress.

Notes

Notes

CHAPTER 4

Turning defeat inside out

Notice, notice, notice:
opportunity is everywhere!

> *Master your own mind, and you master your destiny.*
> J. A. Knight, therapist, author, philosopher 2011

When I had hit a point in my life when I had lost everything dear to me - my children, the family home, treasured possessions, my car, sentimental gifts, old neighbours, friends, respect, and my sense of self – I couldn't imagine for a single moment that life would ever be the same again, and in many respects it never was.

Today I would say that in fact my life is far better. My life is richer because I finally know who I am, what I want and where I am heading. My life has improved because I have learnt more through that challenge than any school could have taught me a thousand times. I no longer feel threatened by change, as I now recognise that practically any situation can be turned around to my advantage, if I maintain the right attitude.

You see once you realise that you are in charge of your own inner world, your own sense of direction, your own aims and desires, then there is a whole new world of possibility that seems to open up as if by magic. Opportunity is a manifestation of events, born of passion!

When you choose to take control of your life with an optimistic view, you can literally make a new beginning for a new you.

When I began my new business I dreamt of a new dynamic me being able to stand up in front of hundreds of people and speak with confidence. I saw a different me working with a good business mind in meetings, and an empathic me working in the therapy room.

At home a fun-loving version of my self comes through, whereby I relax a notch or two, and transform into a happy and content relationship mode. This brings together two versions of me working at my best.

You can create this life partition too, just by imagining it with passion and zest and approaching the issues with an optimistic viewpoint.

At this point in life, you may be facing some tough decisions, or you could be stuck in a set of circumstances that lends you little choice. If you are heavily in debt for example, then of course you will know that the situation is out of your control, that you do indeed owe money. However, how you choose to look at it, and deal with it is something that could work to your advantage. Let's see how, by using the following example.

We have a panic stricken, worried and stressed person, who feels that they have no control over their life, and in turn worries and loses endless amounts of sleep. Now the result of that worry is uncertainty, fear and stress. The stress alone can cause illness, lack of focus and various other mental and physical problems.

Lack of proper sleep due to anxiety, can also compound the problem, leading to mistakes and lack of concentration at work for instance. This happens when we view only the problem but not the solution, and therefore there is a severe lack of seeing any opportunity, or scope for improvement. Our judgement can become seriously clouded, with a feeling of lack of power or control, which in turn leads us to beating ourselves up for being so useless in the first place.

Over time, all these negative cycles compound into one huge problem, and then we tend to repeat the process once again without even realising. As a result, nothing ever changes for the better, and guess what? We then feel stuck, because we are stuck. We are stuck in a cycle of lack of action and foresight.

There may be fear too, deep down where we do not wish to take responsibility for our situation. Indeed responsibility is a scary word for a lot of people, but the word itself is nothing but honourable. The responsibility for employment, bills, housing, banking, and so on is given to those who have reached adulthood. We have reached an experienced level in life due to what we have learnt from past events.

The word 'responsibility' actually tells us that we have the 'ability' to 'respond' to a situation.

With this in mind, let's take a new standpoint and put the above worried, stressed person back in the driving seat. They realise that they do indeed, owe some money and that it has to be paid back. They take responsibility for this as a responsible adult. They accept that they are in control, and do not panic but instead look at the facts. Maybe they take this opportunity to read up or research all the options, to seek some advice and see this as a way to broaden their experience. They recognise that it isn't always necessary to become involved in the drama, but instead they choose to look for ways to improve their circumstances from the outside looking in, with calmness and detachment.

This outlook may result in looking for extra work or putting the word out with friends. In other words keep eyes and ears open, look for any opportunity for assistance and gratefully receive, and learn from it. Over time, the situation may well improve, and that improvement should be noted for any future challenges.

The above example of debt, is a very common one of course, but how about turning your whole life around? Perhaps you have several things on the boil that are challenging you right now, and you just can't see the wood for the trees. Maybe there is just one big choice that could affect several other aspects of your life, or you have an inner fight going on between what you want, and what everybody else wants, that has been affecting your better judgement.

If you are in the position right now, with a tug of war going on, why not give yourself a break by realising that you can go your own way. If you are in the same boat as everyone else, it doesn't necessarily mean that you want to row in the same direction, and if you do so it doesn't mean that you are a bad person.

Compromise of course is encouraged as a good thing, and can work out as a 'win, win' situation for all. Remember though, compromise is an acceptable balance, so make sure you are happy to do this in the first place, as over compromising yourself can lead to future resentment.

If on the other hand you simply feel stuck in a situation, it may be that you do have a choice, but the choices you would have to make are difficult ones, or choices you don't want to make. If this is the case, it is best to simply be forgiving and understanding with yourself, and try to see what would be the best outcome for your future happiness with honest eyes. In other words, take responsibility for recognising what makes you happy, and stand true to it.

Of course there are times when we are faced with such life changing, tough decisions that it can affect others we love in the most negative way imaginable. It is natural that we would never want to hurt those we love, and that to some degree their feelings should be taken as a priority. However, if you truly are miserable and living with an unbearable situation that is unlikely to change, then you must take responsibility to challenge it rather than continue to fear it. If not the situation could be corrosive, you could develop secret resentment over the years, possibly numbing yourself with denial. The choice is always yours.

When dealing with my own perceived version of 'Sophie's choice' in court, I had to face hard fact, and was pushed into making a choice there and then that would change my world forever.

After I had initially lost both my children in one court battle, my daughter had later decided to come and live with me. This was not accepted lightly by her father, and so I sadly found myself battling in court yet again.

However, the law isn't always as straightforward as you might expect, and to my horror I was advised to fight for just my daughter, as I would probably win: if I asked to have both my children back with me however I was told I would probably stand to lose both of them, as my son wanted to stay with his father.

From the outside looking in, it may seem like a straightforward choice to some, but for me at the time, my heart was being ripped into two pieces. At the time, many thoughts crossed my mind such as could I truly believe that my son didn't want to be with me? Could I be sure that my ex-husband was being completely honest with me at the time, given his feelings? Was this in my son's best interest? What would he think of his mother later on at home? Would he ever be mature enough to realise the truth of the situation I was presented with? If he did want to stay with his father, and he knew I didn't fight for him, would he ever understand why I had to make that choice, and would he ever forgive me?

My heart broke, as my solicitor strongly advised me to only pursue my daughter, and that I leave my son to his own choice, given he was the eldest, and his opinions must be considered. After being given just ten minutes to make one of the biggest decisions of my life, I sadly had to back down for fear of losing my daughter, and I chose to fight for only one of my two children.

After nine previous miscarriages, I had never given up hope of having my children,, and was delighted to have two viable pregnancies at last. For this reason my first born was a special gift to me, and so to be put in the position of fighting for only one child when I loved both dearly, was completely devastating to me.

Although I was presented with an impossible choice, I did what I thought best at the time. I took full responsibility for my decision, with the intention and to my knowledge at least one of my two children would have what they requested To that end, I put my own wants aside, which as adults we sometimes have to do. Yes, I was caught in between a rock and a hard place, but nonetheless, the choice had to be made.

Today my children are grown. Both have a decent relationship with one another, my ex-partner and me. The past is the past, and tough times make for hard decisions, but choices have to be made whether we like it or not, in order for life to continue, and evolve.

So by now, we can see that choice is what shapes our future, and opportunity is that golden word that has possibility held within it. Change is the very nature of life, and indeed the universe, and within that change opportunity is actually everywhere. Whether you are in the right place at the right time or not, this matters a little less when you recognise that opportunity is there for the taking, and will come to visit you again very soon if your heart is open to it. Not all choice is bad, and when you view it as a stepping stone, you can make changes for the better.

For instance, let's just say that you are trying to set up a new business and you pop along to try some local group networking. The negatives might be that you don't know a soul, you're a little nervous, have never done it before, but what if you DO go with a positive attitude, and you are armed with your inner 'antennae' seeking out any opportunity that could arise from meeting any one of the possibilities that are available for you there at the time!

What do you think the result might be? If you can feel and see opportunity as your passport for reward, you may be able to seek out success for yourself in the process, such as meeting someone who is willing to swap details or services in return for yours perhaps. You never know where it might lead, or who they might know.

What if the circumstances are more emotionally serious though? Imagine your child is offered a place at a school attended by some children who used to seriously bully him or her in the past, and that the school has an awful reputation. Could there be an opportunity for you to use your past experiences in front of an appeal panel to get your child into a better school perhaps? Do you have any connections through friends, neighbours or relatives who could help? Could you seek useful information by research? This is a challenge that I had myself, and it is possible to create a positive outcome.

Maybe you have a relationship that is going through turmoil. Is there an opportunity to discuss it with a counsellor for free? Or do you have a sincere friend who has faced similar issues and would be willing to talk it over with you? Maybe there is an opportunity for you and your partner to win a competition for a summer break (possibility just what you need) or a family member who knows someone who owns a small villa abroad, and is willing to lend you a small deposit.

What if you have a sick parent who can no longer care for themselves? You could look at turning that negative around into opportunity for positive change. Maybe it is about time that they had a chance to spend some quality time with you, could you improve your home in some way, so they could live with you and take the proceeds from the sale of their home to fund it? Perhaps you don't have that choice, and yet this could be an opportunity for them to move closer to you into a warden based complex. Maybe it is time they went into a nice home, where there are gardens, and other people of a similar age to mix with. Again, look at the opportunity for a solution, not the problem.

Supposing you had lost everything, your kids, your home, your furniture, your car and eventually even your job due to on-going stress. How would you cope? What opportunity could you find in such a situation? Remember, every situation is part of a drama that you can choose to be dragged into, or to view with peaceful logic and rise above with loving detachment.

There of course are many choices you could make under any of these circumstances, and those choices depend very much on you, your state of mind and your approach to life itself. Your life! If you view each situation as if it almost didn't belong to you personally, and you were trying to help a friend with logical advice then you could save some valuable time, and really be off to a flying start.

Let's take a look at some hypothetical situations you could face. For instance, suppose that you are homeless, you have nowhere to go for whatever reason, and you have no support from close friends and extremely limited means of support from family who have limited room or finances of their own. What do you do?

Firstly of course there is the need to use your inner wisdom and knowledge based on your own values, as pointed out in the earlier chapters of this book. Finding what fits and works for you, who you are, and what you value will be valuable assets in times of future challenge.

Secondly, knowledge is everything, and I am happy to say it's everywhere these days as we live in the 21st century of communication, plus of course it's practically free! Make use of free services to gain insight into your situation and search until you can't search any more! Go to your library, browse through every book you can find that may be able to help, get free internet access for as long as you can through your local library.

Make use of your local town hall services, and look into local charity help and information. Then there are friends and family who may know someone who can share valuable knowledge with you. There are also places like the Citizens Advice Bureau who can help in a myriad of ways. All this help is there for you to seek, and use to your advantage.

Of course information is of no use whatsoever, without action. Action is required in order to get your vehicle to work, the car will get you to where you want to be, but not without the fuel (ie, intent and knowledge) to push the vehicle forwards.

Once you are rolling however, life will start to look a little rosier, but remember that the first gear is always the hardest. Pulling away from an old situation is difficult, but not impossible. Remember, YOU are in charge; you are the No.1 boss of you and your world!

Along the road of your personal journey, at times there may be rain and at others little rays of sunshine, and opportunities here and there. I can give you a few examples of the blessings I have counted for myself. When close friends know of your situation you will suddenly find:

- Unexpected invites for company at weekends.
- Someone's granny has sadly just passed away, and instead of throwing unwanted bits out, YOU were the first person your friend thought of when it came to handing them down.
- People suddenly start presenting you with little home-made gifts. Very touching.
- Offers to assist you in court come forth, others are willing to take half a day off work for you.
- Endless cups of tea, biscuits, time, advice and understanding.
- Physical help with some jobs around the home that you just can't do, due to ill health or inability.

- Offers to lend you things that you don't have right now.

Of course you can't rely on others for everything, and when the chips are well and truly down, there is little you can offer back when funds are low and the stakes are high. However, a simple cup of tea, a warm smile, a hug and a genuine thank you are sometimes all that friends want in order to see that you are happy with their help and understanding of the situation.

If we look back across time, nothing is as bleak as it seems at the time. Remember, nothing ever stays the same forever (as is the nature of our beautiful universe), which is a comforting thought when you are going through uncertainty and personal challenge. Opportunity is something that is available for you to seek out, by simply recognising that it is there. All you have to do is remember that you are in charge of your life, and that you can make a difference.

*From this day
forwards I am open to
positive opportunity, and
know that if I seek it,
I will see it.
I can confidently
rely on me.*

Notes

CHAPTER 5

Letting go, moving forwards

Lifting a weight, living a life

> *Never to suffer would be never to have been blessed*
> Edgar Allan Poe, American poet and writer 1809-1849

Believe it or not, letting go is a completely natural part of life that starts from the very day we are born. From the very beginning we are growing, changing and evolving, and each stage of that change requires a letting go of the old, to make way for the new.

From day one, we leave the physical connection with our

mother's womb to be born into a the new world of the unknown. Then through various stages of our development, we let go of the warmth of breast milk to eventually be fed with solid food. We let go of the safe dependence of a nappy, in order to use the toilet on our own. As we learn to stand and walk, we let go of supports such as furniture in order to stand and walk alone.

Eventually, as we move on, we let go of mother's daily protection in order for us to go to school, and we go on to make new friends and meet new experiences. We continue through early life to release old possessions, clothes and toys, to make way for new growth and education, and so through our entire lives, the list continues to grow.

This means that both mentally and physically we create a pattern of release, and let go of things, people and situations time and time again. Whether it is moving home or leaving an area, our friends at school, our parents, or old possessions... whatever our stage of life, it is a cycle that eventually comes to its natural conclusion, allowing it to begin once again. If you think about this on-going cycle of journeys, if we want new experiences then eventually something has to give way for the new.

So, if letting go is a natural part of growth, why does letting go of the past become a problem when we get older? Why do some people find this such a painful thing to do? After all, if something is no longer serving us, why would we need to keep it?

The problem for most of us in letting either a physical or mental issue go, is usually a deep fear of the unknown, or a strong emotional attachment to a particular person or situation. You see as a child, everything is new and we experience everything for the very first time, and therefore we are eager to move forward, to learn, stretch ourselves and grow. This is why

children in general, although not all, are viewed as fearles
and fun loving!

Children see the world through different eyes, and although
they sometimes see uncertainty, they also see adventure! As we
get older the 'been there done that' mentality can kick in and
hold us back, as we collate past and sometimes painful
experiences as a subconscious lesson to avoid in the future.

We can hold onto past hurts and wounds, a bit like a child
choosing to hold a thorn instead of the rose, thus allowing it to
continue to wound us on a deeper level for as long as it likes. In
time, this wound will (like any wound) fester deep in the
subconscious mind, where it will eventually take sanctuary
beneath various other wounds that have built up over the years.
In truth, we all hold scars from the past, but if you could see that
scar on the outside of your body, and if that scar was causing you
pain, wouldn't you consider doing something about it?

So, what holds us back from emotional freedom?

For most of us, once again it can be the fear of the unknown,
being falsely labelled, cost, embarrassment at how we may react
in front of a therapist – enough for us to put help off for another
day. Sometimes we also kid ourselves into thinking that we are
coping just fine, which is another reason for lack of action.

However, if we are repeating destructive cycles of self-limiting
behaviour time and time again, or if we are reacting in a way to
things that are affecting our working life, relationships or
happiness, then perhaps it is time to think again.

Eventually, there comes a time when we have to take
responsibility for who we are, and how we choose to behave. For
instance, if you know that your past is haunting you, or holding
you back from a positive future, then letting go of your past

disappointments and hurts could help you to feel lighter and take positive action!

For many people, a good therapist or counsellor is a wise choice to make in times of extreme stress, fear and uncertainty, especially if all else has failed. Of course in all cases, there are people who fit in well with certain therapies or methods of recovery, and others who would choose a different way – like anything it all depends on the individual, their life story and their perception.

Take this moment in your life for instance. Today you are sitting down reading this book, and have taken the option to be responsible for your own growth and understanding, and that is a truly wonderful thing! By the time you get to the end of this book, your whole perspective may have altered, or your view of your situation may have suddenly become crystal clear, as you continue to feel empowered. The thing is my friend, you had a choice, an option, and you made that choice, so well done you!

We are not all the same, and so we react to different situations in our own unique way. What if you have a friend or someone you hold dear, who has had trouble letting go of the past? What if someone or something has hurt you so deeply that you just can't seem to get past that disappointment yourself? Can this book still help or be of use?

If your intention is to help yourself, then yes this book will be of positive use to you, and will benefit your new life. However, if there has ever been one issue that I see clients regularly for, it is past emotional events that are negatively affecting their future goals, and they may simply feel that they cannot face the past alone.

For this reason (and without wanting to sound too dull or grave) I would always recommend that if you are having any self-destructive thoughts that are continuing to affect your future well-being, that you seek professional advice in addition to this book as soon as possible.

Let's continue our exciting journey into your future, with this fun little exercise!

Detachment and Clarity Exercise

Remember, life is a gift that is available to all for those who wish to participate in it. If you hold on to past disappointments, mistakes, doubts, blame, guilt or hurts, your life will be all the more painful and less adventurous for it.

So, take your time, put the kettle on, and get a pen and pad now and ask yourself some of these thought provoking gems:

- Is there something I am holding on to from my past that is no longer mine to hold?
- Am I 100% to blame for X, Y, Z situation?
- Did I have any bad intention in mind at the time?
- Do I deserve to be punished for a lifetime?
- Does my own self judgement really belong to me, or someone else?
- What past negative conditioning could be affecting me now?
- If my best friend came to me in tears, would I judge and treat that friend as harshly as I treat myself now?

Now in order to get the very best from this exercise, it is important to answer these questions as honestly and as automatically as you can. After all, there is no one else to judge you, except yourself, and if you are open to change, then forgiveness should be no stranger to you.

Have you finished? Now I want you to look at your list at your own leisure, and try to view the answers as honestly and as kindly as you possibly can. I want you to look at your answers as a best friend would, and see how someone who holds your best interests at heart would see those answers.

After a few moments of looking at your answers from a healthy objective point of view, can you now recognise that you should not be as harshly judged as you judge yourself? Can you see how as human beings the choices we sometimes make can resonate with others in similar circumstances? If not, I want you to do this exercise once again, but this time I want you to imagine your best friend and a guardian angel are looking at the situation with loving detachment. In other words, they will not have the emotional based judgements that you have.

Quick fix exercise

Just imagine that you have handed your concerns over to a best friend, and allow that friend to give their loving advice from their own detached perspective. A beautiful guardian angel is a step further away from your friend, and so is further detached. Both should agree on a form of loving advice for you by the end of the exercise.

This simple but extremely helpful exercise can bring great clarity in times of self-blame, shame or guilt. In any situation there is cause and then effect, and although we should take responsibility for our own actions, it usually takes more than one person, or scenario to create havoc and distress.

Another extremely useful exercise is to simply stand under a shower and imagine that all of your past hurts and disappointments are being washed away. You need a little time alone to just concentrate on feeling all of that dark negative energy washing down the plug hole, as you feel cleansed and alive! When you finally emerge, you will feel a whole lot lighter for it, believe me!

Last but not least, I would thoroughly recommend that you purchase a journal, and treat this journal as if it contained gold dust! A journal is not just a book that holds your feelings, it is a gateway to your soul. When you reflect back on past entries, you will see just how far you have come, and how your thinking has changed and improved. And if not, well you can see where you need to brush up for yourself a little!

I always keep my journal close, and usually write in it at night. I find that at the end of the day, there is nothing more relaxing and uplifting than writing down your thoughts, feelings, plans and wishes, to help you get a good night's sleep. It literally is like lifting a weight off your mind, and putting it onto paper! Funnily enough, thousands of years ago, this is what the Aztecs used to do with tiny worry dolls, that they would place under their pillow at night, with the wish that the doll would find a magical solution by the morning. They knew even then, how to encourage the mind to work well. Try it, you may be happily surprised!

From this day forwards I am willing to release the past, in order to move securely into my future. My future is golden!

Notes

Notes

✳

CHAPTER 6

Finding the dream: a new chapter for planet you

Creating a new reality through infinite possibility

> *Make the most of the best, and the least of worst.*
> Robert Louis Stevenson, Scottish writer and poet 1850-1894.

We all have dreams of an ideal life, and how happy we could be living that dream, obtaining our every goal without a single hitch, but in reality could we really handle that? Some spiritual psychologists firmly believe that we are all in fact exactly where we are meant to be at this precise moment in time. After all, if we weren't we would have changed it right? It's a bit like the comfort zone syndrome, whereby we always end up in one place because it is familiar, because it is all we know, and in that knowing lie safety, certainty and even security, even if that place is a negative one at times.

Let's look at someone who has a past of negative conditioning, let downs, poverty and disappointment, but suddenly out of the blue, they have won the lottery! They simply can't believe their luck – they have won millions of pounds! At first they are elated, because after all, money is what everyone wants isn't it? They may tell family, friends, or maybe tell no one at all, but the feeling of anticipation and excitement is beyond them. When the money is finally delivered to them, it comes with various financial advisors, corporate bodies and media experts, people they have never previously had any dealings with, nor knowledge of perhaps.

After listening intently, they take much of the wise advice, and now are free to do as they wish with their money. Up until now, winning the lottery has only been a dream, but now it is a reality! Oh what to do? For most people, the obvious and most common answers tend to be I will buy a house, have a holiday, buy a new car, and treat the kids, and family... but then what?

I'm not saying that winning a huge amount of money is a bad thing. What I am saying is that the first statement of 'I can't believe it' is what can stand in the way in more ways than you might think. It is actually a negative giveaway to our inner world, as 'I can't believe it' is a statement that almost shouts 'I don't deserve it'. What about saying 'this is a wish come true' or 'this is my lucky day' instead?

As a direct result of you now thinking of the lottery, I want you to open up your mind to possibility! But what I don't want is for you to view the world by other's standards and expectations when they may not necessarily sit comfortably with your own. You see, these days, The National Lottery has a counselling service, yes, a service that is there for people like you and I, but why? Because my friends, when you have no more than nothing, and have been used to nothing, well winning can become a huge burden!

For instance, if you have an automatic subconscious program running, rooted in poverty based thinking, and that program is linked to past negative experiences, then you may go on a massive spending spree and blow the whole lot, out of a fear of not having enough. As mad as this may sound, it does actually happen! Or maybe you will go the other way completely, and deny yourself enjoyment by continuing to work as hard as you did before, saving every penny, or maybe guilt will encourage you to give the lot away to friends, family or a charity, which is wonderful, but what about you?

You see, depending on how we perceive ourselves, we tend to lean towards emotional drivers and preconditioning from past influences, which is why it is so important to STOP and ask... Is this truly what I desire?

The example of the lottery has been chosen here because I want you to think about a future full of possibility, a future where the question would be... If I were to always succeed what would I do? If I had endless income what would I enjoy, or offer? I want you to start opening your mind to infinite possibilities because there is a very important reason for doing so.

If we didn't have people who were open to possibilities we

wouldn't have any of the luxuries that we enjoy today. If nothing was ever discussed, thought of, invented, hoped for, aimed for and fought for against all the odds, well what a sad and boring bunch we would all be!

So today it is your turn to open up your mind and enjoy the feeling and openness of possibility. It's your turn to look into yourself at a deeper level, and remember what games you played when you were just 5 or 6 years old, and why you enjoyed them so much. It is your turn to recall when you were 8 or 9 and you first became interested, or good at a particular subject at school... why did you love it so?

You can think again of when you were in your teens, what influenced you? What did you love? Who did you want to be, and why? And finally, when you were in your late teens approaching your twenties, what skills had you acquired by then? What interested you? What did you dream of and why?

Throughout life, we have all had different experiences, influences and occurrences that shape the way we are today. If, for instance, you wanted to be a racing driver at 5, and then enjoyed assembling meccano at 7, became good at maths at 13, and wanted to be a pop star at 17, then you have a good indication of who you are, what makes you tick and why. So, if you won the lottery now, what would you do? What would you really love to do that says something about you?

If you were involved in ballet at 5, dreamed of horse riding at 7, became good at English at 8, learnt to make people smile and laugh by 10, and became involved in drama in your teens, what might you enjoy today? What career would you like to be involved in, and why?

Naturally, if a woman in her thirties hasn't attended a ballet class since the age of 9, well she isn't going to be a professional ballerina today, but she could ask herself what was it about ballet that she loved? Was it the dressing up, freedom of movement, showmanship, expression, involvement? All of these questions will reveal more about the central core of you, your inner child, than any other questions that you may have asked before, and in that lies the answer to your own truth and happiness.

The reason for us looking at the above questions is simple. They are intended to put you in a place of truth in order to pin down your real goals, happiness and future potential.

Today is the first day that you have encountered what lies on this page, today is a day when you have the opportunity to refresh your mind with new aspects of you. Today you are living in possibility, and in that possibility lays infinite empowerment!

When we see things clearly, we are less burdened and feel lighter as a result. When we have made a decision based on our own truth, we don't live a lie, and therefore we give ourselves more energy to move forward with hope. You my friend, have the power to turn your life around and shine an inner torch on what you wish to focus. What you decide to aspire to is your choice, and yours alone, so be proud of who you are. You are a survivor!

In finding our dreams and desires, we also find what we value most. As a valid human being and individual, you are responsible for how you decide to run your life, and within that life, its meaning.

No longer do you have to worry about 'fitting in with the herd', because you are courageous enough to live your unique truth, and to find out what makes you a happier and more content person, who isn't afraid to ask the big questions.

What does your life mean to you at this moment, and what could it mean to you in the future? If you wish to have fulfilling and loving relationships, then set a goal to learn all you can about relationships, and become who you wish to be. If you wish to be financially successful, then talk to successful people, ask questions, find websites and books, that will tell you all you need to know. If you want improved health, then seek out those who are healthy, learn their secret, join their clubs and eat what you know will be of benefit to you, and help you to shine from the inside out. We are all responsible for our own outcome, given how we choose to live and what we feel we deserve. What we include in our lives will ultimately create our end result. It is never too late to take action and apply positive change.

So ask yourself this empowering question: what small difference or step could I make today that would eventually create a positive future for me? Just think about it, take your time, and when you have answered it you can begin to look at the bigger picture, the end result of what you are aiming for.

Today is a powerful moment in your life, today is in the now, and starting from now is where you can create a more fulfilling future for you, and for those you love.

By seeing this vital moment as a stepping stone you can learn so much more about what is important to you. Most of us just worry about immediate results, without giving much thought to the long term which can be far more satisfying and rewarding. I always think of politics when I say this, because most politicians and councillors are looking for results in the now, dealing with what they want as soon as possible, but sometimes without looking at the long term implications. In short they are simply fire fighting.

We live in a society of the 'quick fix' and as most of us already know, the quick fix is something that will just do for now. Of course there are times when we need to take the shortest route possible, when there is an expectation or urgency to get instant results. However, when we are faced with something that is important to us, our needs and our truth, then planning, nurturing and looking at the bigger picture will always serve a more positive outcome.

So, with a bigger picture in mind…Just imagine if for today, you could move away from everyone you know, and recreate yourself. You could be any version of you that you wish to be. Imagine how the new you would handle different challenges, ideas and situations, and how the new you would choose to dress, stand, talk and look. The possibilities in a new version of you are endless. If your hair is blonde for instance, you could choose to go dark; if your posture is poor, you could choose to stand tall. If you are meek in your manner, you could step into an assertive version of yourself. How do you think this would make you feel?

If you could wave a magic wand today, and change just one thing in your life, what would it be? Just think about it for a second or two.

The above question is one that I use quite often in my clinic with various clients, as it is a direct and extremely empowering question. This is because it challenges you to search for a truth, it directs you to what you value and it holds you responsible for the answer.

Of course, if your answer was to simply 'win the lottery', then money is your priority As for actually winning the lottery, well it is possible, but you may have a long wait. The next step would be to determine what responsibility you're willing to take for this goal, and what person you're willing to become in order to attain it.

So let's take a look at how we can create a more powerful person within, to shine in the outside world.

Not so long ago, I had a male client who was fantastic at

asserting his authority in the workplace. He was also amazing at giving speeches, and being the funniest man at weddings and parties. When it came to tenderness and understanding however, he just couldn't quite cut it.

Over time, this became a big problem for him and his family. For instance, when his little girl cut her knee quite badly and was crying, he would simply tell her to get up and stop making a fuss. When his wife was upset because of bereavement he would tell a joke, in a vain attempt to make her smile, as he felt awkward reaching out to offer her his warmth, sympathy and understanding. When his own father died, he could not show how he was feeling at all.

This made him an extremely miserable guy, who was unsurprisingly beginning to get the cold shoulder from some of his family, as they simply took his response as cold, uncaring and slightly unnatural.

In truth, deep down he was a sensitive man. Sadly, he found feelings difficult to express, not just because of his direct personality, but due to his past conditioning too. You see, he had come from a family of direct communicators, who were more fact based and less feeling based. This was the way they operated. His mother and father worked hard, but had little time to hug, praise or cuddle him – in fact they never touched him unless it was for punishment, instruction or correction.

This man's parents were not evil or nasty; they were simply practical, hardworking, logical, direct, and living in an era that held little respect for 'mummy's boys', or anyone who was perceived to be soft. So, he just had to fall in line. With his working class background if he was perceived as being soft, he would become a permanent target for bullies.

Now I'm not saying that all people from a working class background are hard and uncaring, as I was born into one of the poorest areas in west London back in the late 1960s, on a council estate at the top of a huge tower block, but I have a different outlook. We all deal with things in different ways, given the personality we have, and the conditioning we have inherited, which is sometimes based on fear, anger and deprivation. Over the years, our conditioning can simply become an acceptable inner part of us that turns into habit. Sometimes we are wise enough to question this habit, and sometimes, if it is not noticeably destructive, then we do not.

In this case, the man in question was wise enough to realise that it was destroying his family relationships, and he was clever enough to go and do something about it. At the end of his session with me, he had discovered that he had viewed caring people as weak, silly, time wasting and soft, all due to his past conditioning.

We all know this is not true, as most nurses and doctors, school teachers, nursery staff and those in the caring professions will tell you. To be caring is actually quite challenging. It can carry the burden of self-sacrifice, hard work, long hours, determination and the mental ability to see things from another's point of view, all while putting your own needs temporarily to one side.

The client in question went on to work on and develop his caring side after realising the strengths of his inner nurturer personality. As a result he could comfort his daughter and his wife, while receiving the love and affection he actually needed for himself – a true win/win situation.

Now I wonder if you could do the same for yourself?

The short answer is yes, of course you could, because like most of us, you can choose to make changes if you want to, and you can start right now – all you have to do is visualize that positive change in the first place in order to create what you want.

Firstly, I want you to take stock and to recognise an area of your life you are really unhappy with, stuck in a rut with, or just aren't getting the results in that you want. Start off with something small for now. For most people this bit is simple, as dissatisfaction is quite easy to detect.

To give you an idea, imagine for a moment that you find it hard to confront your boss. You find it easy to be naturally caring and loving, to be chatty and outgoing, but you find it difficult to assert yourself and be calm enough to process ideas in a logical fashion, when faced with conflict with your boss, or any other type of conflict for that matter.

Obviously assertiveness, confrontation, and logic are the areas that you would prefer to brush up on. This will help you push yourself forward, get results, maybe climb the career ladder, express your ideas in meetings and achieve other professional goals.

What personality type do you think you need to be to achieve this? I am sure we can already envision that person in our head – they are assertive and have no problem with confronting any situation calmly and confidently in a controlled and logical manner. They are confident because they are calm. They think clearly because they use a logical point of view, not an emotional one. They are also probably aware of their posture, and will stand correctly to assert their authority, and they may dress accordingly, in a plain but professional way. These are the character traits of the assertive person.

Our exercise can hold the key to this problem. First we need to notice the issue itself, (I'm far too emotional, and avoid confrontation). Next we need to know what it is that ideally we would like, (to be calmer in difficult situations, assertive and logical). Then we visualise that character trait that we want to have over and over again, and finally we step into that role when it is needed, in order to step into a calmer version of ourselves.

In other words, if we need to be fully equipped for any situation, then we are already ready for it, firstly in our minds, and then in our actions. Preparation is the key, just like a dress rehearsal.

So, you can be anyone you want to be, ready for any situation at any time. You and you alone have the power to change your world. You are the creator of your own reality, and truth, and you are the one who already knows the values you hold dear, and why. It is you who knows your own history, and it is you who can choose to use that history to your advantage. Anything is possible, if we feel we have the ability to overcome our challenges.

As unique human beings, we all have our own potential. We can choose to sink into submission, and allow life to wash over us, or we can rise above those waves and take the ride of our lives! Which would you rather do?

*From this day
forwards I choose to
spread my wings fearlessly.
I live in infinite possibility!*

Notes

Notes

CHAPTER 7

Embracing change, living the adventure

Experiencing the light

> *When it is dark enough we can see the stars*
> Ralph Waldo Emerson, American essayist,
> poet and philosopher 1803-1882

I remember that during my most challenging times of debt, loss and bereavement, I found it difficult to find a way out. All the problems that I had at that time, seemed to fill a vast bottomless pit, which I was sinking deeper and deeper into by the minute.

The mess I felt I was in seemed so uncontrollable that I couldn't untangle myself at all. Every time I reached up or out for help, it felt like I was just slipping back down again, and to some extent I was.

Then suddenly, after taking just one small step at a time in the right direction, and continuing to focus my energy on what I wanted, rather than what I didn't, I awoke one morning and finally saw the light. It was as if a weight had been lifted off my shoulders, and optimism was a gift that had come to visit after a long, dark night.

All I had room for was possibility, and within that was my new motivation – all because I had never given up hope, not for one minute, not even during my darkest hour, hope kept me going, and hope kept me alive, even when it was just a faint glimmer of hope in the distance.

To some, I may have come across as just a wishful thinker, a dreamer, a nomad who had lost touch with reality, but today I am still standing – I am successful, happy and in touch with myself.

Your light may be just around the corner, or may have switched on within you already, I hope. You know by now that you are just as deserving as the next person, and your needs are just as valid. When you realise that nothing ever stays the same forever, it is almost a comfort – all things can and will change eventually for the better.

I like to use the term an 'ah ha!' moment. A time when you finally realise that you are back in the driving seat, and that you can make a difference, even if it is a small one. It's when you begin to see your future clearly, and can identify your dreams and goals. As Austin Powers would say 'I've got my Mo Jo back baby, Oh yeah!'

Life is an adventure for you to experience and the beauty of it is that you don't need loads of cash to do it. Because when your light is switched on my friend, so is your creative thinking ability.

For me, my 'ah ha!' moment sent me a strong and serious message. The message was to WAKE UP! It was as if I had previously been bogged down with so many losses, so many hurts and challenges, I had lost my way, and had even lost a sense of me, what I stood for, and what I wanted. I was totally lost and in the dark. I didn't know who I was.

When I finally shook off the darkness that had surrounded me, I could finally begin to see clearly with a new perspective, and take back direction of my life. With this in mind, my new journey of self-discovery began, and that discovery started with adventure.

To me adventure was like a new medicine. I wanted to try it, and experience a new way of living, just to see what would happen as a result. The first thing I did was to write a list... a list of all things possible and even things that seemed impossible at the time. My list of dreams was born, and written as if this was my last day on earth, and I wanted to cram in everything I could.

To give you an idea of the kind of things you might include on your list, here are some of the things that were on mine:

- Jump out of a plane at 10,000+ feet
- Have a tattoo or two
- Completely change my hair
- Go to the National Ballet
- Go to an open air opera in Rome
- Get a soft-top sports car
- Own a cute Beetle Bug
- Ride in a hot air balloon
- Start my own business

- Create a fab website
- Write my own book
- Have a Harley Street clinic
- Break an arrow in half on my throat
- Go to belly dancing lessons
- Walk on hot coals for charity twice in a row
- Travel beyond Europe
- Take responsibility for arranging my own holiday and catching the plane myself
- Decorate, pay for and organise my own home alone, bills and all
- Go horse riding and learn to canter
- Swim with dolphins
- Hold a baby tiger cub in my arms
- Sleep with Cherokee Indians in a tepee under the stars
- Hold a variety of snakes including a beautiful python, and a chilli rose tarantula spider in my hand
- Give a speech to over 500 people with ease
- Be interviewed on live radio
- Have my own radio show
- Appear on a TV chat show
- Publish a self-help magazine column
- Create my own charity
- Set up an emotional awareness program in schools and colleges
- Offer reduced therapy vouchers, for those on the poverty line, making therapy available to all
- Have my own high street walk-in clinic offering therapies for all

And so the list goes on, and can go on for you too. I am always adding things to my list and have experienced over half of these so far, but all things come in good time when we live our lives with possibility!

So now, I would like you to take a pen and pad and have some fun, allowing your imagination to run wild. Don't think too much about what what you are writing at this time – just allow your mind to open as to what life has to offer. Think of all the experiences, negative or otherwise you have had to date, and how you would like to stretch future experiences into a new dimension. Create your own ideas, pinch some of mine too if you like, but just get those possibilities into your mind, and down onto paper.

If you are stuck, then here is a list of A to Z examples to get that creative mind working...

Abseiling, Belly dancing, Car racing, Deep sea diving, Elephant riding, Flying lessons, Go-karting, Horse riding, Ice sculpting, Jet skiing, Kayaking, Land Rover Experience, Mountain climbing, Nature watching, Ocean cruising, Parachuting, Queuing to be the first, Rambling, Star gazing, Theatregoing, Underwater shark cage experience, Volunteering, White water rafting, X-Box gaming challenge, Yachting, Zoo-keeping or whatever else tickles your fancy.

If you've done that, that's great, but if not, then don't worry, it will come. Even if your list is just a small one to start with, it is still an achievement when you open up your mind to possibility. From this moment on, your ball will start rolling, and rolling in the right direction.

So, now that you have had a little time to think, and write down your dreams, goals and ambitions I want you to take a step back and digest what you have written. Some of you will be surprised at what you have put down, and you may even ask yourself, 'is that really me on that piece of paper?' And some of you may not be too surprised. Either way it doesn't really matter, but what does matter here, is that your list is now in existence, and it belongs to you.

You may ask 'so what's the point of all this?' The point is you now have something on paper that is written by you, owned by you and a possibility for you. At this stage in your life, it is neither here nor there whether you have the time or money, as events can surprise us from time to time. You have opened up your mind to new experiences that you would like to enjoy.

If you are still wondering how on earth you would gain a sports car, a trip to the Royal Opera House, or a parachute experience, please allow me to explain how your change in perception can hurry these experiences along, even when you have no money in real terms, and are recovering from debts, loss and recent challenges.

Not long after my extremely sticky and complicated divorce, I was left with next to nothing in material terms. I had no home, no furniture and no car. All I had left was my little part time job which paid me a modest salary, along with some housing benefit, which was just about enough for me to survive on, and that was it.

At this time however, my life was beginning to change quite rapidly. I had taken steps to improve my life, and I had eventually arrived at a place that while not outwardly ideal, looked as if the world was opening up to me. I was in a place of possibility, regardless of my on-going challenges, and belief made all the difference.

To begin with, I had received next to nothing from my divorce settlement, but was that wasn't going to deter me from making positive changes to my new found freedom.

I knew that I needed a car to travel to work, but I didn't want just any old car, not after having such a miserable time, – no, I wanted a bright red soft-top! I needed to cheer myself up and keep my positive approach, plus I wanted to have the new experience of driving a sports car.

I was determined to achieve this first goal and instead of buying a lottery ticket each week, I decided to invest my pound coins by saving them up in an old coffee jar, along with any other spare change I could lay my hands on down the back of the sofa.

I also kept my ears and eyes open, joined the library where I could get free internet access, looked on eBay and various other websites, putting the word out to friends and family that I needed a bargain buy. I even cut out pictures and made myself a dream board, including lots of images of little red sporty numbers, so I could stay on target, and remind myself of what I was aiming for each day. A good friend suggested that a little MX-5 might be a possibility as they are reliable, small, great fun and tend to keep their value.

After a few months of careful saving and positive thinking, my friend emailed to say he had found a little red MX-5 sports car for just a few hundred pounds more that I had. Ok, it was over 10 years old, but this little baby turned out to be well kept, with just a few tiny holes in the hood here and there, and other than that she was in great shape, beautifully polished, regularly serviced, and she ran like a dream. This fantastic car even had a button for pop up headlights, like a matchbox toy car I had when I was a little girl... it couldn't have been more perfect, I loved it!

Just a few weeks later I had my new car. I had sold old clothes, put every coin away in my jar that was possible, and went just a little overdrawn with the bank, but my first sports car experience was mine. And I owed it, old or not, I owned it every nut and bolt. I had the first thing on my list, and had proved to myself that dreams can come true.

Excited, I continued my journey with anticipation. Around that time, I also decided to look into parachuting for charity, as this was a way that I could help others, and get my jump for free. All I needed to do was raise some money for charity, and help raise awareness for cystic fibrosis in the process. I went about raising money in the office where I worked – it took me just over four months of asking various colleagues, friends, neighbours and family, but I did it, raising over £487.00 for a cystic fibrosis charity.

On the day of the jump, all I could think of was how lucky I was to be there to experience a jump. To my added delight I was introduced to a lovely man, who showed me the ropes before strapping me onto him for the jump. The experience itself was truly amazing and something that will stay with me forever! Plus he was a bit of a hunk… well what can I say?

Since then I have also done fire walks for charity, as well as offering my time for pampering days for cancer charities, and for those who are carers for their sick and terminally ill relatives. All these have been rewarding and amazing experiences, and I have met loads of great people along the way.

After my car and parachute experiences I was now facing Christmas, and finances were tight. I had started to dream of seeing the ballet at the Royal Opera House, but the tickets were impossibly expensive for me at the time. This wasn't going to deter me from achieving my goal, and so I looked into the possibility of getting them by alternative means. This thought took me once again to an online search at the library, and so I found the phone number of the Royal Opera House.

With some degree of anticipation, I rang the number, and asked if there was any way a single mother could get tickets to take her children to watch the ballet. At this point, I was half expecting a no, but as my good old Gran used to say, 'If you don't ask, then you will never know.'

The answer I got astounded me. They did offer discounted tickets as an educational and cultural offer for single mums and underprivileged children, plus my daughter could go back stage with a friend, try on a variety of ballerina outfits, and have photos taken too!

Note: I must add that this offer was back in 2006/2007, and I sincerely hope it is still available. If you want to find out, then all you have to do is ask, just as I did. It will be your first voyage of discovery...

At the time, I couldn't quite believe my luck. I was totally filled up with gratitude and pride and so I seized the opportunity with both hands. I was so pleased to be able to take my daughter, as she had recently come back to live with me, but sadly my son was absent as he was still living with his father. So my daughter took a friend of hers, and two young girls had the time of their lives, with outfits tried on, their photos taken and memories of a wonderful ballet at Christmas time. Who'd have thought it was possible?

You see, if we seek then we shall find, and if we ask then we will receive the answers that we need. If we see something as an opportunity with optimistic eyes, then the world seems almost like a treasure chest waiting to be opened.

There are many other little lucky things that have brushed up against me during some of my darkest hours, and I always try to keep a note of them. Regardless of how big or small, if my deepest wish is even half met I feel immensely grateful. It makes no sense to constantly look up and push myself forwards, if I don't stop to notice or smell the roses along the way.

With blessings in mind, I want you now to just take some time for yourself, and tally up all the things you can be grateful for today (regardless of what challenges you are facing) even if they are some of the smallest things. Here are some examples which may vary from person to person:

- I woke up this morning, with the ability to experience another day.
- I have good health, or better health than those who I know are suffering currently.
- I have friends, family, colleagues or neighbours who I can get in touch with at almost any time, and by almost any means.
- The trees, grass, flowers and fresh air are available to me, to view, touch or smell.
- I have food in my cupboard and clean water in the tap.
- I have a roof to give me shelter.
- I have clothes on my back to keep me warm.
- I have some cherished memories to keep to myself, if I choose to remember them at any time.
- I have a mind that works, and it will support me each day.
- I can take a warm bath or shower to cleanse, relax or refresh me.
- I have a place to sleep and put my head down when the day has been challenging.

Listing our small blessings is extremely important, as we often take such things for granted. If you take the time to read them, you will see that all of our basic survival needs are met: food, warmth, shelter, water, clothing and community. Take away just one of these things, and we begin to panic. Take away two and we will begin to truly suffer. Take away three and we may well begin to perish.

We are lucky to have so much more than previous generations ever had, and life will continue to develop in more ways that we could possibly imagine. If we look back to just over 100-200 years ago, the problems our ancestors faced were far more harsh, destructive and downright physically challenging then we would ever recognise. The good news is that because of them, you are here today, a true survivor of previous tough and resilient ancestry! Well done to all those who kept on going before you, because you my friend are at the end of a long line of true survivors!

Remember, all that have gone before us have faced fear, challenge and adversity, and despite that, you are the evidence that a better future is possible!

From this day forwards
I choose to see what I
have to be grateful for.
My gratitude uplifts me.
I am grateful to be alive!

Notes

Notes

CHAPTER 8

Staying strong

Being true to you

> *To be what we are, And to become what we are*
> *capable of becoming is the only end in life.*
> Robert Louis Stevenson, Scottish author and poet 1850-1894

*F*or many of us, when we have a future in mind, and the light has finally switched on, then there is much to celebrate. When we have a focus, and we have pushed our worries and concerns to one side, then we finally have the clarity that is needed to actually start getting us somewhere.

However, many people have one tiny concern that rises to the surface, and what a common concern it is – 'How do I keep on going?' In other words, where do you find the motivation needed to keep on track?

Without motivation, focus is lost. Motivation is the fuel that drives us towards our goal with vigour and energy. If you look the word up in the dictionary you will see the word comes from the Latin 'motivus', meaning to move forward.

Let's think of an old car that has sat on the driveway and has rusted a little over the years. Maybe that car has been neglected to such a point that it is now only a shade of its former self. Once upon a time, this car was shiny and new and vibrant, but now it is rusty, old and neglected with flattened tyres, and nothing in the tank to take it anywhere.

Then one day someone spots this little car, and notices its true potential. This car is unique, and like any car it is designed to go places, to travel around, have fun with, and be of service. With this in mind, the new owner starts paying their full attention to the car, and sets about making the necessary repairs to it, so once again it can be of service.

Over time, the new owner may add little bits and pieces to the car to enhance its performance, and may even improve it cosmetically, as they are now seeing, feeling, and wanting to live in the possibility of having great fun with this new car. Once the car is taken out into the sunshine in all its glory, the owner jumps in and takes it for its first ride around the block.

All is going well, and so the owner decides to challenge his new project, and takes it on a longer journey. During this journey the car faces motorways, windy roads, traffic lights, jams, pedestrians, and various other obstacles, and copes perfectly, until it is faced with a steep hill. It suddenly loses its oomph. Now perhaps that oomph can be added with extra fuel, a lighter load, fine tuning or adjustments, but what if it can't? Will that little car ever be able to conquer that steep hill? Or is it destined to languish on the driveway once again, and rust away into nothing?

What a shame it would be for that little car to have gone all that way, only to fail at the final hurdle. Over that hill there may be a beautiful beach or destination that the owner had decided he wanted to sit and rest at, enjoy, and relax with his new purchase. After all, the whole idea was to enjoy travelling around and enjoy reaching new destinations in the first place.

This is a bit like a person who has been given a new lease of life. They have decided to take control of their destiny by recognising that life doesn't just happen to them, but rather they have choice, giving them a renewed sense of truth and control. Just as you are in control now.

That person then sets about making their own repairs to their life, and lo and behold they improve beyond doubt. Then comes the day that they set about moving towards their goals and dreams, in other words their personal 'destination', and so they set off on their journey, fully repaired, and willing to move forwards.

Throughout many obstacles on their journey, they continue towards their dream destination, until that is they hit their large hill, or whatever challenge it may be. Their fuel may be low or it could be that they feel they simply don't have the oomph to carry on, or keep on moving.

This is when we need to draw on our reserves, our inner strength, and our natural ancestral survival skills, and ignite that passion with renewed zest. But where is my zest, I hear you shout! Don't worry, it is there if you dig deep, it is there or you wouldn't be here.

So, go ahead and dig deep, and connect with your inner spark of passion, your fuel for survival, your drive for success, and keep on moving, rolling onwards and upwards, because you are a miracle of nature, a perfectly built biological piece of art, with all its learning abilities, internavigational skills, mathematical accumulations, linguistic programming, logic, creative ability, problem solving, nerve endings, muscles, fibres, cells, membranes, arteries and any other part of the wholeness of a human being.

The word human being conjures up someone who is living in the possibility of being themselves, and living in truth. They are part of something bigger, and they can be by themselves, or belong and be with others. We have the intelligence to grow, to learn and to aspire to whatever we choose.

So, with all those wonderful thoughts in mind, let's take a look at what floats your boat, ticks your tock, wags your tail, pushes your fun button, and makes you want to get up in the morning. Now this is the fun part...

Once again grab a piece of paper to make a list. On this list, will be all that drives you, all that gives you inspiration, and all that you value most highly. But before you start writing anything on that list, I want you to sit quietly and think whether what you value is true to you or not. This is extremely important, as sometimes we are falsely conditioned into thinking that certain things should or ought to be important to us, when they may not be.

So, just for a few minutes or so, I want you to think back. Think back to your earliest memories if you want, and just think of all of the 'shoulds' and 'oughts' that you were told. Now, as an adult with your own opinions and experiences, question those beliefs. Be totally honest with yourself, because there is no right or wrong here, just simple truth.

After writing your list, you can go away and have a nice hot cup of tea, and when you come back to review what you have written you will suddenly see in truth, what you tend to truly agree with, and what you don't.

Now, I want you to examine any beliefs, past conditioning and even family sayings that you no longer entirely agree with, and as you notice how your view has changed over this time, you may now also realise that you have grown, or are at the very least beginning to grow into a stronger version of yourself. In other words, you are coming into alignment with the true you. So enjoy this experience, and discover as much as you can about yourself, with an open and honest heart.

Here's an example. A friend of mine knew a lady who used to place her roast beef in the oven tin each Sunday, with both ends sliced off, even though there was plenty of room in the tin. When she was asked why she cut either side of the beef away, she simply replied, 'well, that's what you do with beef.' When questioned why that was and after a few minutes of thought the lady replied 'because that is what my mother did'. When further pressed and after much continued thought the reply came with a sudden 'ah ha!' moment, when she said 'ah because my grandmother's meat tin was too small to hold the joint!'

The above example shows us perfectly how preconditioning works, when we simply do not question the whys of that conditioning, and carry on regardless without question.

Back to the exercise. After a little while, you should have more of an idea what you do agree with, and what you don't; what you would love to do and why, and what you wouldn't; what you do love, and what you don't; along with any fears and old outworn beliefs that once belonged to someone else, who may have passed those beliefs onto you. So now that you have a clearer picture let's see how that truth can be of benefit to your future.

The true you comes from the very depths of your being, your soul, your centre. When you act in truth, suddenly you may feel lighter, as if an unnecessary load has been lifted from your shoulders and you have a sense of true freedom in your choices. When living your truth, thoughts may begin to emerge in a clearer fashion, and decisions as a consequence will become easier for you to make, as you live with clarity.

When things are clear to us, we have the ability to see where we are going, what we want, and how we wish to make the right choices for us, not someone else but us, our personal truth, our personal choices. It is almost as if you are living in perfection, with a purity of thought that is so clear that any fears or doubts are just something that used to belong to somebody else a long time ago.

Naturally there will be times when we are challenged, fearful and scared, but those times needn't be as traumatic as they have been in the past. Because by changing your state of mind, you now hold power, and that power is in living within your truth. In fact, you are taking a step towards freedom, and to be free takes a trusting and fearless person. Guess what – you are that fearless person! A true survivor, who has faced up to who they are, recognised who they are, taken full responsibility for who they are and accepted who they are. You are now more than ready to freely take that bull by the horns, and move into your own arena of personal excellence. Congratulations for being so blooming fabulous – well done you!

From this day forwards I am free to make my own decisions based upon my own truth. I am free!

Notes

Notes

CHAPTER 9

Living with positive intention

Keeping the vampires at bay

> *With our thoughts we make our world*
> Buddha, Indian religious teacher and founder
> of Buddhism c. 563-483 BC

It's human nature to have varying moods – days when we are up and days when we are down. All aspects of life have positive and negative sides and most of the time we hit a 'somewhere in between place', an equilibrium, where we can say we're content.

Within this familiar middle ground we have learnt to get by. We may start our day getting out of the wrong side of the bed, but we will continue to aim for that comfort zone, that equilibrium. If we start the day in the most amazing mood, or have had some fabulous news, then that high is a great feeling, but as we can't stay on that high for 24 hours a day, once again we will aim for our familiar equilibrium.

The familiar is a safe place, we can rely on it, and that is fine if you are content with just that thought. For a moment though imagine that instead of feeling safe within your equilibrium, you could also feel really good about yourself. What if you could feel as if you were guiding your day, instead of your day dictating to you the usual expectations of the same old day.

To some extent we will always come up against certain occurrences – like queuing in the post office or getting stuck in a traffic jam – and we do learn to notice them in order to prepare ourselves for next time. Yes there are imperfections in life, and yes there will be down days, but we do not have to be a slave to those occurrences. Sometimes it can seem as if we have no other option, we have no choice, and we are a victim of circumstance.

To some degree, yes that is true. However, nothing is truly out of your control. Of course, we all understand that things in life can get in our way, but we also have things that we would like to happen instead, so the things that we would like to happen should not go unnoticed. Because we are all valid human beings, what we want should be recognised and taken into account.

This brings me to the topic of energy. Energy is what makes the world go round, energy makes things grow, energy gives us light, heat, and if you count the Earth's magnetic field as energy it also gives us our gravitational pull. Energy travels, and energy gives power. In science we learn that energy can't be destroyed: I believe that could make energy eternal.

Now what if I told you that we also have our own unique energy code? Each person has a different code and different levels of energy. For instance, have you ever met a person who seems to have endless bags of high energy? Or met a person that just doesn't seem to have any go in them whatsoever? This could be down to a medical condition, but what if it isn't? (I always maintain that if we don't ask 'what if' often enough, we will all turn into mindless drones. So go ahead and ask 'what if', teach your children to ask themselves 'what if'. This one little question can open the door to endless possibility and learning)

Now as we head into this world of energy, I want you to pay close attention because this is important. From now on I want you to recognise how your energy affects your mood, and the world around you. I want you to make the most of what you have, in order to get the best results for you.

If you can imagine that same day again, coming out of work with a feeling of dread at the thought of the looming traffic jammed journey home, just take a moment to feel what is going on inside of you. Ask yourself if your mood and low energy affects your world, and if it is doing you any good.

If you now imagine a different scenario where you feel less of a victim of circumstance, but more of leader of your own fate notice how you feel now. In all probability you will feel energised.

Ok, so now let's take some positive new energy and apply it to your own inner world. Feel that sense of empowerment, and notice what thoughts may cross your mind. Instead of the usual dismal acceptance, you may have just ignited a flame to light up your situation, or you may have noticed something that no one else has. Try it! After all what have you got to lose?

If you approach this from an energetic, positively charged perspective, any of the following could be the result. You may suddenly decide to opt for an alternative route, which may turn out to be the best decision you have ever made... you may think of leaving work a little later, after doing a bit of leisurely shopping... or you may decide to fill a flask up with a nice hot cuppa, turn the radio on in your car and just go with the flow... and all the while your positively charged perspective will alter your world, alter your mood, and ultimately alter your results.

The same goes for other people too. Have you ever spent what seems like the longest hour ever with a person who is like the darkest cloud constantly looming over you? Some people are just so draining. In fact they are almost like energy vampires – you are left with next to no energy or a permanent headache after they are gone. At other times, we meet people who leave us on a high. We may feel fantastic for no apparent reason, but they just tend to give us a lift. How many other people do you think would like to spend time with this person... how many others would like to feel that lift after a hard day too?

The two scenarios above are perfect examples of energy transference, and of how our own energy and the energy of others can affect us, and the world around us, to such a extent that it can affect our whole mood, or even day.

So what can we do about this energy transference, and how do we get the most out of it. Well, to put it into simple terms, take notice of who you spend your time with, and why. Now I am not saying for one moment that we should abandon those in need, or those who are in a weak situation because they are down, but if you are not in a position to handle that situation, as it may drag you down too, then don't partake in it.

If on the other hand you are on such a high that you can spare your energy and replace that energy again for yourself, then go ahead my friend, have fun lifting up and giving!

If, for example, you are visiting a friend who tends to drag you down, in all probability what they are unintentionally and unconsciously seeking is a little 'feel good' energy for themselves. Now some people can be a little greedy and will take and take, and sap the energy from others, just because they either can't be bothered to try and do it for themselves, or that they are too weak or ill to do it for themselves.

Please understand that it is not your job to allow someone else to offload, whinge or moan themselves into a whirl of negativity, just so they can offload that negative matter onto you. If you are in a strong position, then if you can handle it that's ok, but if you are not having such a great time of it yourself, or are in the middle of some self-healing work, then do yourself the biggest favour – politely make an excuse, and stay away.

In times of darkness, we need some light. In the bleak winter of our journey the last thing we need is more bleakness. If you are looking for a lift, then look for the sunshine, the light. Surround yourself with upbeat successful people – after all they are successful for a reason. Try and gently take some of that lovely energy for yourself, and repeat what lessons you have learnt from them in a positive way, so that you can replace that lovely positive energy anywhere, anytime for yourself. What a wonderful gift!

As time goes by, you will notice how much better life seems to be. Things suddenly seem a little brighter, and more in balance or control. Your life forms around your wants and wishes, and because you are in such a positive state of mind, you are grateful and notice how grateful you are for what you now have, even if it is just a great feeling. It's all good stuff, and the more you get of that good stuff the more you will want.

Material things and abundance will tend to come to you in one way or another, sometimes in the strangest of ways. Take my situation – when I had lost everything and had nothing but a bin liner or two to my name I suddenly had a stroke of very natural luck. After lifting my mood out of the pity party mode and into the onwards and upwards mode I found offers of various types coming out of the woodwork.

Simple yet valuable things, such as a girlfriend offering to view some apartments with me one Saturday afternoon. Her support and high energy gave me everything I needed for a positive result, and I found a great two bed maisonette, above a lovely old couple who were helpful and full of wonderful energy. They proved to be perfect neighbours too! Bless them.

Not long after that I had various offers of bed sets, cutlery and towels just to get me going... an old ironing board and even a microwave were heading my way too. Then came an old Ford Escort, (ok, so small mammals used to overtake me going uphill, it had rust, and it smelt of damp washing) but it was a start, and I was so grateful. I got that little car for fifty quid and it saw me through in the initial days before my divorce came through.

After a year or so, my daughter came to me, and announced that she wanted to live with me. So we moved into a rental house with more room for her, and my son to stay over at weekends. I was so happy to have her, but I had nothing at all from my previous rented maisonette in way of furniture.

However, the new house I found was just as I had imagined... I had spent many a night consciously and subconsciously trying to alter my energy into a higher state, a thankful state, and the house we moved into was just perfect for us. It had almost everything on my list of hopes and wishes, with ample room for my son to come and stay. I wondered what I would do about furniture, but once again lucky energy helped – my uncle was moving in with his new girlfriend and so he donated many items from his home. Already our new home was forming, and I didn't care if it was second hand or not.

The point I am making here is the following – is luck, just luck? I believe it has it something to do with the flow of energy that surrounds us. If someone has a history of bad fortune, they are not necessarily destined to that for the rest of their life.

This is why it is so important to take stock, and to forgive others as well as yourself, and then to try to move forward with a positive intent, as best you can. After all, if you can't forgive yourself, you will find it hard to get any positive energy that will work for you. In other words, if you are not on your side, then your energy won't be either!

If there was ever a time for us to gather our thoughts together and dig in, then this is the time. With the recent news of recession, rising petrol prices, wars in various parts of the world and worries for many a parent, we need to dig deep into our resources, to bring about the most positive results.

Yes, there will be times when things get tough, or when we will hit a low ebb, and despite the wonderful examples I have given above, I also had other things going on that were not so nice. The difference was, I didn't choose to focus on the negatives, but instead chose to stay on track with my optimistic hopes and wishes, and took action when opportunity came my way.

When you look at your ancestors, and how they triumphed over adversity, without a clue about the energy that we have discussed here, they had little chance of succeeding without a natural positive force of determination and focus. Today we have so many luxuries such as clean running water, electric light, food, technology, education, national health support and alternative health products should we wish to seek them out.

I could go on, but I am sure you see my point. We have so much more to hand than our strong and resilient ancestors had. Today, you may have a different type of stress to combat, but the tools are there for you to overcome it. Today life may be lived at a faster pace, but you choose that pace. Today the media may dictate that looks are important, but you choose how you wish to look, how you wish to identify yourself, express your dress, and who you want to be. Take your power now, and find your truth, because within truth there is the comfort of what is real, and what is not. In truth, you can come home to yourself, and dance to your own song at your own pace, and not to the song of others. What a relief that can be!

As a final word to close this chapter, just take notice of how people around you operate, and you will soon see for yourself the outcome of different attitudes and the reflective energy of their actions. You will begin to see how the simple cause and effect of energy works for us all.

*From this day
forwards I recognise that
I am deserving of a
fabulous future.
My positive energy feeds
my outlook!*

Notes

Notes

Notes

CHAPTER 10

Sending yourself flowers

Remembering you, receiving reward

> *A bit of fragrance always clings*
> *to the hand that gives you roses*
> Chinese proverb

As human beings we have the advantage over the rest of the animal kingdom for we have the unique gift of sentient intelligence and creativity. We continue to focus on how we can progress onto the next level, whether that level is a stronger building structure, a better type of car, or even inventing a smaller piece of technology for the sake of convenience.

Since time began man has striven to better himself in many

ways. When man decides that life can be made easier by using a different route, or that there is a higher reward waiting for him if he makes certain improvements then he will take that necessary action. Those improvements can also lead to easier circumstances. As I have mentioned earlier, life is a lot more comfortable today than it was 100 years ago for our ancestors.

This progress affects our world on an everyday basis. Well for most of us, we never get the time to invent something new, let alone even have the head space left to think about it – what with being told this, being sold that, endless emails and paperwork, trying to pay our mortgage or rent, getting the week's food shop in, putting a wash on, and 'ooh it's Auntie Jan's birthday soon, better get her a card', and 'oh yeah I forgot to book an appointment to see the doctor about my stomach trouble'. And then there's work, and so the list goes on.

With each and every passing day, we need lists of this and that, when we have to get things done by, and how. Alongside all of this we may have a demanding family or responsibilities towards an elderly neighbour or friend in need. There may be increasing pressure on us at work too, or in some other area of our life. Then there are physical or mental health issues for some, making time for appointments, or having to give more thought to their diet, or lifestyle choices.

The message here is that life in the 21st century seems to be more stressful, busier and more confusing than ever. The question is, are we really busier than our mothers and fathers were before us? After all, we've invented labour saving devices such as microwaves, washing machines, dishwashers, vacuum cleaners, hair dryers, cars to make way for more 'me time'.

We often don't seem to benefit from that precious me time.

Perhaps we have less time to really think, and more physical time left over these days. As a nation we are becoming more obese, according to recent health reports, and health problems are on the increase, so why are we thinking so much when we should be doing and what are we thinking about when we could instead be taking action.

For a start although every invention has a positive side, it also has a negative side. For instance, television can be extremely entertaining and educational at times, but it can also stop some of us from taking a walk, or going out with the family. Even for the elderly it can be a life saver for loneliness, but it can also stop them from making the effort to do something a little different for a change, or to apply themselves to something that could benefit them in a new way.

A computer game is a great way to relax after a hard day at work, but what if we switch off and go into a dream world a little too much. A washing machine gives us free time to do other things while it is washing our clothes, but do we make good use of that time or do we worry about what we need to do next? A car will take us from A to B, but doesn't encourage us to walk or cycle anywhere at all.

Sometimes the use of technology is a must and can't be avoided, but at other times it can also be a serious hindrance to our physical wellbeing. We are continuing to strive for what will make life easier, more comfortable and demand less physical effort.

In reality the effort has not ceased, as with every technological gain, there is a whole new requirement for learning and adapting to that gain, and re-learning the new way of doing things requires mental effort. Even new offers from supermarkets, mobile phone shops, energy suppliers, all require extra mental energy, as we are bombarded with a mass of alternatives, which in turn is just adding to the confusion.

Confusion comes from constant change, where we don't have any chance to settle into a routine, but instead are being thrown the next offer, or even the next change to local parking arrangements via the council, the next rule in work ethics, the next rule in teaching methods, and so on.

Change is a necessary part of life, and man is built for natural progression to strive to bigger and better achievements for the wellbeing of community and personal development, but is that change meant to move at such a demanding rate? Such constant transition means there isn't a chance to truly understand what has just passed.

The lesson comes from the journey, and nature is currently giving a big clue as to how that journey should proceed. Right now there is a major shift in climate going on, that we have known about for a great many years, and for a great many years before that our planet has been in transition to this new state.

Like a bud that appears in springtime, a flower will not appear until the conditions are right. Like an arm that has been fractured, it will not heal until it has been given good time to do so. A solitary leopard that hasn't eaten for days cannot feed herself or her young until she has spotted, stalked, caught and secured her prey, and all this knowledge comes from the journey before her.

When we apply this to our lives, we can also look at the bigger picture and work backwards to the present day, and in doing so we can then begin to see what steps need to be taken for a better future. Although we live in a competitive world, the immediate reward is something that will just tide you over, and isn't always the best solution for long term rewards. Now that we have

examined this concept, let's take a look at how many o
in today's world we live in.

We already know that although we may not get all of what we
want done because of mental distraction or stress, we are
nonetheless creatures of progression who need to plan for a
better future. On a small scale we can look at a young couple who
are going to move in together and see how planning for their
future begins to take shape. This may include:

- Opening a savings account for a deposit for a new home.
- Looking for a better paid job, or permanent position.
- Wanting to progress within a job you are already in.
- Taking on extra evening work.
- Beginning to collect ideas for home furnishings from
  magazines etc...
- Building up a picture in your mind's eye of what kind of
  property you would want and where.
- Starting to ask for advice from friends and relatives for
  inspiration and direction.
- Looking around estate agents, and in property papers.
- Looking for cheap deals on insurance, energy etc...
- Any further steps such as an engagement ring, a new puppy
  or having a family...

This list could be endless, but hopefully you will begin to see
just how much mental energy we put into our daily lives, before
we even consider taking any action, and these things will naturally
take time to develop. Things and plans take time, and the moment
we think everything should be instant (like our coffee) is when
we set ourselves up for serious disappointment.

You have come a long way on your personal journey to this point in time, and for that you should be extremely proud. We are not in a race after all, and if you think that you are no further along that path right now than you were a year or so ago, then think again.

Unfortunately more than half of the issues clients present to me in my clinic are a sense of despair in their lack of self-perception and progress. The expectations people place upon their own shoulders are sadly in line with the supermarkets, the internet, and everything else that is expected to be instant in our community. In reality nothing is instant. Everything has an order, everything has a time to develop, and to evolve, and that includes us.

Your emotional state and any serious negative preconditioning can take up to three to four times longer to heal than a broken arm or leg... or that serious childhood abuse issues could take even longer. So you can see that to expect so much from yourself is unrealistic.

Of course not everyone is the same, but do notice how healing isn't always instant, and how it naturally isn't meant to be. Sometimes we just need the time to reflect, learn and relax into our own healing... and to do this we need time.

So, next time you feel that you aren't getting ahead, progressing fast enough, or that you feel snowed under, think again. I want you to instead send yourself flowers, give yourself a treat of some sort and truly recognise the fact that yes, you have come further than you think. I want you to try this easy and fun little exercise. So go on and grab yourself a drink and settle down with a journal or pad.

The Five Year Challenge

I want you to think back to around five years ago, and regardless of what you were doing, or where you were at the time, reflect upon any concerns, problems, challenges or issues you had at that time... any issues at all. Write them down on your notepad. Well done.

Now at the bottom of those notes, write:

THESE WERE MY YEAR 5 CHALLENGES.

Right, now underneath those challenges and issues I want you to recall as best you can how you dealt with those concerns, and how you managed to overcome any of them. You don't have to have dealt with all of them, as we are being realistic here. When you're done I want you to write:

THESE WERE MY YEAR 5 APPLICATIONS because the way you dealt with those challenges, was how you applied yourself to them at the time.

Fantastic! Now I want you to do exactly the same for three years ago, and then one year ago, and when you've finished come back to this page.

Well done for putting in this valuable time and effort, now we are nearly there.

Finally, I want you to acknowledge from year five backwards any achievements or gains that you made, in between the challenges you had. This could be that you took an exam or a new job, that you had a baby, that you purchased your first car, home, decent piece of furniture to your own taste, travelled for the first time to a lovely place, gave a best man's speech for the first time, or experienced something different for the first time. Whatever comes to mind, I want you to note down.

In completing this exercise you should now be able to see for yourself, just how resilient and competent you really are, and in doing so you will see just how far you have come. You will also see for yourself how you arrived at this point today, and you'll notice any patterns within your life history. Again, you may have thought of things that you have gained along the way, such as any extra knowledge or wisdom, material goods, unique experiences from your own perception, or personal achievements.

When we look into our own history, we sometimes fail to recognise just how far we have come, and how many obstacles we have faced along the way. By reflecting on our ability to overcome obstacles, and by reminding ourselves of our inborn resilience, we are in fact underlining a truth. That truth is that as a survivor we are already in safe hands and those hands belong to us!

Yes, you are here today because of you. Beyond every circumstance, you have proven that you have the ability to cope with life's challenges, and with every passing day your wisdom and strength is increasing.

In this book, it is my sincere hope that I have made a difference from a refreshed perception, for a more positive outcome to your future hopes, dreams and wishes. From personal experience, I have swallowed many a bitter pill from some of life's harshest lessons, and read many a book in the pursuit of further knowledge, wisdom and growth.

It is now that I ask you to truly send yourself flowers, and to once again, never forget just how far you have come, and never to undermine the journey that you have made so far. Don't rush too far forward to the next thing, before you have stopped, acknowledged and given thanks for who you are, and how you have blossomed.

I wish you a pleasant journey...

From this day forwards I recognise that I am deserving of wonderful things, and I am proud of who I am! I am safe to be me!

Notes

Notes

Final word

As a final word

As we draw to a close, I would like to thank you for reading this book. Not all of us have a chance to start over in life, but all worthwhile journeys begin with just one small step at a time. It has been a pleasure in sharing my experiences, knowledge and insights with you, and in doing so I sincerely wish you well in all your endeavours for a brighter future, full of success, joy and happiness.

Love Joanna

X

Acknowledgements

Finally I would like to thank the friends who were with me during some of my darkest hours. Thank you to:-

Christine Carter, June Daniels, Kam O'Donnell, Nicky Howe, Mandy Smith, Enza Breen and Deborah Fife for your love, understanding and support.

Pat Rance, Mel Cucuzzella, Nicky Howe and Enza Breen for your kind donations of home bits n bobs, when I didn't have a single item.

Peter Smith for his furniture donations and help when I didn't have a bed to sleep in or a chair to sit on.

Dad for helping me to decorate my first flat, for polishing my car, bread, milk, advice and endless cups of tea.

Mum for lending me your sofa for weeks on end, your advice and kind support when I was homeless and had nowhere to live.

Roy for always keeping it real.

Liz Everett, Loretta Quinn and Murielle Maupoint for their support and encouragement in my decision to write this book.

And finally to the barefoot doctor for being a fantastic source of fun and inspiration!

Bless you all x

To the many others that have shared your time, a kind word, a smile, and a cup of tea... you know who you are... thank you x

About the Author

Joanna Knight began her amazing journey into the world of Clinical Hypnosis, NLP and mind mechanics back in 2006, after a combination of difficult life challenges and personal change. It was this that led her to an interest, and on-going study of spiritual philosophy, and the psychological effects of stress on the human condition.

Joanna soon realised that her journey wouldn't stop there, as her new insights and passion for human excellence continued to drive her forward.

It wasn't long after this that she realised just how powerful the mind can be in the face of adversity and challenge. From this perspective Joanna continued to view and monitor her own inner world, as well as that of others, with a renewed curiosity and perspective.

Today Joanna is a successful business woman having started her own business from scratch as a single parent with little more than a shoestring budget. From these beginnings, Joanna delivers her practice from three clinics, including Harley Street London, and has run her own local radio show, aided local charity events, presented motivational talks and continues to develop educational courses on stress management for teenagers and adults alike. It is her dream, to motivate and empower everyone she meets, and to allow them to see for themselves, just how phenomenal the human psyche can be.

Her heartfelt discovery has now led to a more fulfilling life, full of possibility, freedom and success! It is her wish, that this success is shared with you.

For more information on Joanna Knight's Events, Workshops, Seminars, Group Therapies, Corporate and One to One sessions please contact Joanna at Joanna@1stsuccess.com or visit www.1stsuccess.com.

An Inner Light
That Shines So Bright

By Liz Everett

**Available from Amazon,
www.liveitpublishing.com
& all good bookshops**

A Heart Warming Collection of Inspirational Writings

An Inner Light That Shines So Bright is a heart-warming collection of inspirational writings that will capture your imagination. Use the powerful words in this remarkable book to:

- Lift your spirits and energise your soul
- Bring comfort, joy, happiness and light into your life
- Enhance personal reflection and meditation
- Encourage your creative inner self to emerge

These emotional and intuitive writings, inspired by Nature, Angels, Faith and Healing amongst others, will touch the heart of everyone in some way.

'Liz shines her light with radiant simplicity, expressing both her sorrow and joy in a way that touched my heart. I felt moved, uplifted and inspired as her experiences resonated with my own, nudging me further forwards on my inner journey.'

Patsi Hayes, Author of Anusha Healing

'These poems cover the spectrum of life: from the joy of nature, to love, faith and painful feelings of loss. I am sure that they will bring insight and inspiration to others who have the pleasure of reading them'.

Dr. Tony Avery, Professor of Primary Care, University of Nottingham

'Liz's passionate poetry is compulsively readable... providing one with an opportunity to read between the lines and hence sending them on the profound journey of self-discovery.'

Dr. Eva Carlton Ph.D. BSc (Hons) Psychology

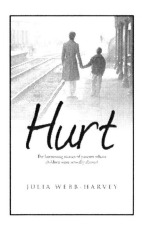

JULIA WEBB-HARVEY

The harrowing stories of parents whose children were sexually abused

Hurt tells the deeply moving stories of parents after they discover their child has been sexually abused. Julia Webb-Harvey beautifully narrates and facilitates parents' exploration of the truly horrible experiences –the devastation, struggles and crushing isolation - and how they set about remaking their own lives and those of their families. *Hurt* tells it like it is, tackling the social taboo of childhood sexual abuse.

"At last , thanks to Julia Webb-Harvey, a book written by experts through lived experience on the plight and courage of loving parents, who face the trauma of their child's abuse, often caused by their own partner. A must for survivors and clinicians alike."

Dr Valerie Sinason is a writer and psychoanalyst

"Hurt is an important book, which faces up to the reality of childhood sexual abuse. Hurt gives hope that families can recover, and will be a massive support to any parent/carer suffering the fallout of sexual abuse."

Denise Hubble, Clinical Services Manager, Mosac.

Lightning Source UK Ltd.
Milton Keynes UK
UKOW05f1056021014

239501UK00001B/5/P